What Leaders are Saying About *Signs of Life*

"I have been privileged to have Ken Johnson as my pastor, mentor, and friend for 16 years. Wise teachers and writers like Pastor Ken are extremely rare and immensely valuable. He has the gift of being able to take complex, controversial, and emotionally charged concepts and explain them simply and conversationally. He brings them to life, just as he brings life to every situation and to all who are blessed to know him. As you enjoy each page of this book, you can expect fresh insights and inspiration as Ken unpacks the secrets of life."

–**Michael Sipe**, Founder of 10x Catalyst Groups and
Bestselling Author of *The Avada Principle*

"Ken Johnson is my longtime friend, in ministry and in life. Ken is a natural teacher, whether he is hiking mountain trails or playing sports or preparing sermons, he is a keen observer who is eager to share what he sees and learns. Our ancestors were called hunter-gatherers; Ken is a hunter-gatherer who searches for and shares God's wisdom. I invite you to walk the path of this book with him to experience what he has discovered about 'The Signs of Life.'"

–**Dr. Cliff Hanes**, Pastor, District Supervisor, and
former Denominational Vice President/Missions

"Would you invest in a daily five minutes of life-infusion that could alter your worldview? Five minutes, perhaps with a good cup of coffee? This book offers just that in a thought-provoking and stimulating look at principles recorded by John the Apostle, a close personal friend of Jesus. Ken's life-application stories, along with humor and challenges, will incentivize you to embrace God's invitation to a better, stronger, longer life. Who doesn't want that?"

"We have had the privilege as leaders and elders of watching Ken

Johnson live out these principles before us as our senior pastor at Westside Church in Bend, Oregon. Ken and this book are the real deal!"

–John M. and Sonja G. Decker,
Authors of *Doing What Jesus Did* and *The Ambassadors Series*

"*Signs of Life* breaks full life down to simple truths based on the book of John. Ken has used vibrant stories to take us on a journey of discovery in excelling in everyday life. It is jam packed with God's truth to uncover your gifts, talents, and tools by investing just five minutes a day.

Signs of Life is a must read for anyone who feels there is more inside them and wants to live a more passionate and purposeful life."

–Dirk Zeller, CEO Sales Champions,
Author of *Success Habits for Dummies*

"Ken Johnson is a brilliantly gifted pastor and writer. Ken's five minutes a day study of the gospel of John illustrates the simplicity of having more of Jesus in your life. Ken brings to life the Word with thought provoking explanations and daily challenges. It's totally different from any other study guide of God's word that I've seen, and I guarantee (I'll reimburse your cost of book) it'll have a PPP (profound, practical, positive) impact on your life!"

–Mike Tennant, Owner, Tennant Developments

"Our kids began riding their bicycles with training wheels. What initially had helped them would eventually hold them back. Ken Johnson, the author of this devotional on the Book of John, won't let us keep training wheels on. He helps us see that time, training and tenacity are required to grow beyond them. Get ready to soar!"

–Glenn Burris, Jr. President, The Foursquare Church

"Kim and I have known Ken for over 35 years. In the faith-centric world of pastors, leaders, and evangelists, Ken has remained firmly rooted in a life of moral discipline and passion for the pursuit of the Father's presence. Ken powerfully reflects the beauty and majesty of the King and he is truly one of the best men we know. His tremendous heart for straight-forward, biblically sound, clear-cut communication of the Gospel is richly evident in his latest book *Signs of Life*. Get it. Devour it. Live it . . . because it is the truth of God's Word."

—**Troy Meeder**, CEO and Cofounder of Crystal Peaks Youth Ranch/Refuge Ministries and Author of *Average Joe* and Kim Meeder, CCO and Cofounder of Crystal Peaks Youth Ranch/Refuge Ministries, and Author of *Hope Rising, Bridge Called Hope, Blind Hope, Fierce Beauty*

Signs of Life

God's Invitation to a Better, Stronger & Longer Life

KEN JOHNSON

Copyright © 2020, Ken Johnson

All rights reserved. No part of this book may be used or reproduced by any means, graphic, electronic, or mechanical (including any information storage retrieval system) without the express written permission from the author, except in the case of brief quotations for use in articles and reviews wherein appropriate attribution of the source is made.

Published in the United States by Ignite Press.
www.ignitepress.us/

ISBN: 978-1-950710-38-6 (Amazon Print)
ISBN: 978-1-950710-39-3 (IngramSpark) PAPERBACK
ISBN: 978-1-950710-40-9 (Smashwords)

For bulk purchase and for booking, contact:
Ken Johnson
info@muchmorealive.com
https://MuchMoreAlive.com

Because of the dynamic nature of the Internet, web addresses or links contained in this book may have been changed since publication and may no longer be valid. The content of this book and all expressed opinions are those of the author and do not reflect the publisher or the publishing team. The author is solely responsible for all content included herein.

Unless otherwise indicated, all Scripture quotations are taken from: The Holy Bible, New International Version®, NIV®. Copyright © 1973, 1978, 1984, 2011 by International Bible Society. Used by permission of Zondervan Publishing House. Scriptures marked (NKJV) are taken from The Holy Bible, New King James Version © 1984 by Thomas Nelson, Inc. Scripture quotations marked (TLB) are taken from The Living Bible, copyright © 1971 by Tyndale House Publishers, Wheaton, Illinois. Scripture quotations marked (NLT) are taken from The New Living Translation, copyright © 1996, 2004 by Tyndale Charitable Trust. Used by permission of Tyndale House Publishers. All rights reserved. Scripture quotations marked (KJV) are taken from The Holy Bible: King James Version. (1995). (electronic ed. of the 1769 edition of the 1611 Authorized Version). Bellingham WA: Logos Research Systems, Inc. Scripture quotations marked (MSG) are taken from The Message, by Eugene Peterson. 1993, 1994, 1995, 1996, 2000, 2001, 2002. Used by permission of NavPress Publishing Group. All rights reserved.

Creative Team: Larry Libby, Louis Dvorak, Jan Mathers, Linda Johnson

OTHER BOOKS BY KEN JOHNSON

Life² - The Life You Were Created to Live
When it All Comes Down it All Comes Down to This - Live in God's Love

CONTENTS

INTRODUCTION:
A BOOK OF LIFE

INVEST FIVE MINUTES a day into becoming more alive....

Years ago, I caught a bullfrog with a fishing pole and a monofilament line. I had attached my big golf-ball-sized bobber at the end of the line. Carefully casting the bobber out in front of the frog, I wiggled it a little and waited. With first one eye and then the other, the bullfrog stared at the wiggling bobber. Finally, he did what I knew he would do. In a flash, he opened his mouth as big as Rhode Island and swallowed the whole thing.

What an appetite!

It doesn't work that way when it comes to following Christ. You might have a very large desire to grow in your faith—even the appetite of a bullfrog—but you can't swallow a whole new life in one gulp. That's why God gave us years, months, days, hours, and minutes. As a matter of fact, each 24-hour day contains 1,440 minutes. Would you be willing to invest five of those minutes in learning how to become more alive?

If that sounds inviting, let's dive into the gospel of John together—day by day, page by page, verse by verse. John is a book about life. It's all about how to live deeper, higher, fuller, sweeter, and richer than ever before. It's a book about the most alive person who has ever left a footprint on this planet. **In him was life (John 1:4a, KJV).**

Life isn't only in Jesus, He invented it. The apostle Peter, at considerable risk to his own neck, stood in front of a hostile audience and declared Jesus to be **the author of life. (Acts 3:15, NLT).**

The gospel of John tells us how to actually get the *life* that is in Jesus Christ into us. The book you hold in your hand breaks John's gospel into five-minute, bite-sized truths about ALIVENESS. Each page, based on just a few words from John, ends with a personal invitation—a challenge to invest one minute in thinking about a life question, concept, challenge, or action. Brief excerpts from the Bible, the book of Life, will appear in bold-faced type without quote marks around them. My hope is that each five-minute investment will yield a rich return on the other 1,435 minutes of your day. As a matter of fact, the bottom-line return on your investment might very well exceed your wildest dreams.

Richer, larger, better life.

24/7…365…forever.

Life Action: Get your hands on a good Bible translation and pick the best time to invest what may become the most important five minutes of your day.

1

IN THE BEGINNING

EXPOSE YOURSELF to radiant life today....

John 1:1

Not long ago at the dentist's office, they took a set of x-rays of my teeth. That momentary exposure to radiation was good for me because it gave the dentist a picture of the true condition of my teeth. Before they snapped the pictures, however, they placed a heavy lead vest over my chest. Why did they do that? Because too much exposure to x-rays can make cells in your body go rogue, which isn't a good thing at all.

As I read through the book of John in the Bible—even in five-minute increments—I am exposing myself to *Life*. John put it like this: *Before anything else existed, there was Christ, with God. He has always been alive and is himself God (John 1:1, TLB).*

John says that Jesus Christ has always been alive and always will be alive. That's pretty amazing, because most of the aliveness in my experience gets nibbled away by deadness—and eventually goes terminal. So along with John, I'd like to expose myself to the radiant life of Christ, the life force that never fades, diminishes, or dies. I'm talking about the life that gets inside me and transforms me from the inside out.

With this particular radiation, however, there is no such thing as too much exposure. John says that the closer we get to Christ and the longer we stay close, the more alive we become.

John starts his book off in an audacious way. He says that before human or animal aliveness began, there was another Aliveness—the ultimate source of all other life that ever was or will be. John's gospel begins with the same three words as the book of Genesis, the very first book of the Bible: *"In the beginning."* John speaks of Jesus as a Being who was 'being' before human beings were 'being.'

I got so attracted to this idea of unstoppable aliveness that I decided I'd read John's book one sentence at a time, hoping to get exposed to the same aliveness he experienced. Want to join me?

Life Question: What book, person, or group of people could I spend time with, in the hope of being exposed to contagious aliveness?

2

WAS THE WORD

FIND THE WORDS that contain contagious aliveness....

John 1:1

I love words.

Words are amazing—and pregnant with ideas. They're walnuts in the shells waiting to be cracked open.

In his gospel of life, John talks about "the Word," the most alive person who has ever lived. He says that when everything else began, the Word already *was.* **In the beginning *was* the Word... (John 1:1).**

The word W-A-S is an existence word. To say that someone *was* means they *existed.* Things that exist do so in the present, past, or future. John says that when all of creation was in the "will exist" category, this "Word" already existed. This person that John calls "the Word" existed, exists, and will exist. He was, He is, and He always will be.

In Greek, the language John used to write his gospel, the term he uses for "word" is *logos.* Logos is defined as "word," "reason," "logic," or "plan." In Greek culture, theology, and philosophy, logos is the divine reason implicit in the cosmos, ordering it and giving it form and meaning.

Jesus Christ—The Word—is God's logic, reason, idea, purpose, or meaning. Christ is at the root of everything that was or ever will be.

Jesus was, is, and always will be God's ultimate idea. God's passion and plans are contained in a Man called "the Word." God spoke life into existence in the beginning using words. Jesus is the ultimate word, the very Word of Life. All things were created for Him, through Him and by means of Him.

Life Question: What is your favorite word, and what ideas does that word contain?

3

THE WORD WAS (WITH) GOD

LISTEN as a dynamic Trio sings a song of life.

JOHN 1:1-3

John refers to Jesus as "the Word." During three years of talking, walking, laughing, and living with the Son of God, John became convinced that Jesus was God's message to us—telling us who He is and what He is doing.

In the beginning was the Word, and the Word was with God, and the Word was God (John 1:1).

Words are the tools we use to communicate. We start with an idea, then dress-up that idea in certain words, so that the person we're talking or writing to can share our thoughts.

Jesus is the Word because He perfectly expresses who God is, what He is thinking, what He is doing, and why He is doing it.

Christians speak of the Father, Son, and Spirit as the *Trinity*. The term doesn't actually appear in the Bible, but the concept runs all through its pages. God the Father, God the Son, and God the Spirit; three in one. Is He three, or one? The answer is "yes."

If Jesus, then, is "the Word," who are the Father and the Spirit? You might look at it like this: God the Father is the Speaker, the *source* of the idea. Jesus is the Word, the *expression* of the idea. The Spirit is the *breath*, the air that carries the spoken word. So what do you have? A Speaker, Words, and Breath. The Eternal Trio tells the story of Life.

How can "the Word" be *with* God and also *be* God? It's the mystery of the Trinity. God is totally "true to His word," and everything He says truthfully expresses who He is. Jesus is that expression—that message from the very heart and mind of God.

Speaking of words, John wraps up his gospel with a purpose statement, explaining why he decided to write it: *But these [words] are written that you may believe that Jesus is the Christ, the Son of God, and that by believing you may have life in his name (John 20:31)*.

Life Challenge: Like God and like John, you can use your ideas, words, and breath to share life and encouragement. Do that intentionally several times today.

4
NIGHT LIGHT

LOOK CLOSELY for signs of life in the dark.

John 1:4-5

Last December, I had a date to duck hunt with a friend on the Willamette River. Leaving my home in Central Oregon at three in the morning, I had intended to meet up with him at six am on a certain gravel road where we would park and walk to our hunting spot.

Arriving in the Willamette Valley, I had the not-so-bright notion to take a new route to our hunting spot in an attempt to save a little time. Bad idea! By 5:45, I had to admit I was lost. It was dark, rainy, and foggy, and I had become completely disoriented. Finally, I saw a sign that said "Unionville—2 miles" and realized where I was. I turned around, headed south, and arrived at our rendezvous in the nick of time. We set out our decoys in the dark and hid in the blind. Later that morning, several ducks might have wished that I hadn't seen that Unionville sign!

What if there were signs—like yellow road signs in the night—pointing to a longer, stronger, better life? Would you put your headlights on bright and look hard to see them?

In him was life, and that life was the light of men. The light shines in the darkness, but the darkness has not understood it (John 1:4-5).

In the first few verses of his Life Book, John calls Jesus "the Word." Here He calls Him "the light." Jesus is presented by John as audio-visual aliveness. In another letter, John wrote of Jesus:

That which was from the beginning, which we have heard, which we have seen with our eyes, which we have looked at and our hands have touched—this we proclaim concerning the Word of life. The life appeared; we have seen it and testify to it, and we proclaim to you the eternal life, which was with the Father and has appeared to us (1 John 1:1-2).

John calls Jesus *the* life, not just *a* life. Then he goes on to call Him "the eternal life." Let that sink in for a moment.

Eternal life isn't a thing, it is a Person.

Life Question: What do the descriptive terms *life* and *light* tell us about the nature of God?

5

LIGHTHOUSE

REFLECT life.

JOHN 1:6-9

When I was ten, our family vacationed on the Oregon coast at Newport. I remember being mesmerized by the lighthouse near the inlet to the bay. My parents explained how a small, centrally located light source in the lighthouse gave off light that was reflected and intensified by hundreds of mirrors.

I like the way Eugene Peterson, author of a brilliant modern-language paraphrase of the Bible called *The Message*, describes a human mirror named John the Baptist:

> *There once was a man, his name John, sent by God to point out the way to the Life-Light. He came to show everyone where to look, who to believe in. John was not himself the Light; he was there to show the way to the Light (John 1:6-8, msg).*

I have a friend who was the lead pastor at the First Baptist church here in Bend, Oregon. I jokingly told him that the true "First Baptist" was John the Baptist. John was called "the Baptist" because he baptized people. But even though John may have been "the first Baptist," he was willing to play second fiddle. He didn't want everyone looking at him, because he knew he was the reflector, not the Light.

> *The Life-Light was the real thing: Every person entering Life he brings into Light (John 1:9, msg).*

Back when I was in high school, I remember trying to find a safe port in my spiritual midnight. I was in the dark spiritually, headed for the rocks. Just then some Life-light reflected off a friend named Steve, who privately challenged me to come back to God.

> *The Life-Light blazed out of the darkness (John 1:5a, msg).*

Steve was like John the Baptist. He knew he wasn't the light; he simply reflected the light. Not too long after our conversation, I negotiated myself across the bar and into a safe port. I will be eternally grateful for that light reflector and hope with all my heart I can be that for others. What better thing could I do with my life?

Life Action: Before you go to bed tonight, think back over your day. Can you remember any moments when you reflected eternal light?

6

BLINDFOLD

REMOVE blinders.

JOHN 1:10-12

John the Baptist understood that his primary mission in life was to reflect the radiant Life-light of Jesus Christ. Five times in the gospel of John he is called a "witness." He wanted people to recognize that Jesus was God's flesh-and-blood invitation to aliveness.

John the author had the same purpose. The words *witness, judge,* and *truth* occur over and over in John's gospel. John writes to provide evidence that Jesus is both life and light. He also realized that light can be reflected or rejected. Speaking of Jesus, John said this: *He was in the world, and though the world was made through him, the world did not recognize him. He came to that which was his own, but his own did not receive him (John 1:10-11).*

Closing my eyes or wearing a blindfold doesn't convert light to darkness, but it does prevent me from seeing the light. Many of Christ's own creations will close their eyes to the brilliant aliveness of the One who *gave life to everything (John 1:4, NLT).*

It's sad to think of spurned light and rejected revelation. But thank

God for the next verse: *Yet to all who received him, to those who believed in his name, he gave the right to become children of God (John 1:12)*.

When we see the light and believe, we receive new life. We are born into the beginning of our true selves. God's grace and our faith carry us into God's forever family and His unstoppable life.

Life Question: If you were taken to court for being a Christ-follower, would a video of your day today contain enough evidence to convict you?

7

MULLIGAN

TAKE GOD'S SECOND CHANCE offers.

JOHN 1:12-16

I'm admitting it right here in print: I've been known to "take a mulligan" in golf.

A mulligan is not just an Irish stew, but a gracious second chance—a new shot at doing things right. It isn't strictly legal or by-the-book, but every now and then it makes all the difference in a game. And although a mulligan represents "cheap grace" to scratch golfers, there is a mulligan mentioned in the Bible that wasn't cheap at all.

Jesus came into time and space from the only eternally alive family: *The Word became flesh and made his dwelling among us. We have seen his glory, the glory of the One and Only, who came from the Father, full of grace and truth (John 1:14).*

John the messenger says that he and his fellow Christ-followers saw the glory of God in Jesus. I believe God's glory to be His brilliant, available ALIVENESS. Irenaeus, the early church father, said an amazing thing: "The glory of God is a man fully alive." Jesus became one of us so that we could become fully alive in Him.

Jesus came to give His life so He could offer you and me a mulligan—a fresh shot at life. Anyone who believes He is who He says He is (HE called Himself "the Life") and receives His gift of deep, unending aliveness, is born into His eternally alive family.

Being alive means being the *true* me, the child-of-God me. It is a process of becoming more and more genuine—and I get another shot at it when my prior attempts roll into the sand trap or rough. This is grace; the undeserved favor of God. But it's not cheap grace. The truth is, obtaining new life for you and me cost Him His earthly life.

> *From the fullness of his grace we have all received one blessing after another (John 1:16).*

Life Action: Think of a time God gave you a mulligan. Why not thank Him again?

8
IN THE DARK

A GREAT LIFE makes God plain as day.

JOHN 1:17-23

John the Baptist was causing quite a stir in Israel. Great throngs sought him out to hear him speak and to be baptized by him in the muddy waters of the Jordan River. For that brief season, he was a rock star. The most famous man in Israel.

It's nice when people think highly of you. Don't you agree? Who doesn't like to be liked? John the Baptist, however, wasn't hyping himself or seeking the spotlight. On the contrary, he was pointing to someone eternal who was about to show up on the scene: *He who comes after me has surpassed me because he was before me (John 1:15).*

The priests and Levites sent messengers to ask John who he was. He responded by saying who he was NOT. **I am not the Christ (John 1:20b).** I guess part of knowing who you are also includes who you aren't. Like the guy who said, "There are two things I know. The first thing is, I know there is a God. The second thing is, I'm not Him."

John, a hot item in his culture in this brief interval of time, said he *wasn't* the Messiah, *wasn't* Elijah, *wasn't* the prophet, and *wasn't* the main attraction. He was, he said, a harbinger and herald, a messenger announcing the upcoming arrival of someone much, much greater. **I am the voice of one calling in the desert,** *"Make straight the way for the Lord" (John 1:23).* Here is one truly amazing thing about discovering God in Christ: The more I discover who He is, the more I discover who I am.

John the Baptist understood that his mission was to point to another person, the Christ. And Jesus Christ came to show us who God is: *No one has ever seen God, not so much as a glimpse. This one-of-a-kind God-Expression, has made him plain as day (John 1:18, MSG).*

I love that! No one has to be in the dark about God. Jesus Christ makes Him PLAIN AS DAY.

Life Action: What is one thing about God that Jesus makes as plain as day to you? Write it down on a piece of paper and think about it three times today.

9

LOOK

BEING HUMBLE = *being more alive.*

John 1:24-38

Ten years ago, God was teaching me how to get free from myself. He clearly (and rather painfully) revealed that I was living a self-centered, self-absorbed life. For the next two years, I said these four words at least once every day: "It's not about me." At first glance, that statement appears to be self-restricting, but it certainly wasn't for me. This new viewpoint progressively freed me to focus on God and on others, knowing that God loved me and would take care of me. It changed me from being someone who came up to a person and thought *Here I am* to a person who came up to a person and thought *Here you are.* I still need periodic re-sets, but my whole new view of life has pretty much changed, and it's made me more alive.

John the Baptist turned the spotlight off of himself and onto Jesus: *The next day John saw Jesus coming toward him and said, "Look, the Lamb of God, who takes away the sin of the world!" (John 1:29).* And it wasn't just a one-time thing for John: *The next day John was there again with two of his disciples. When he saw Jesus passing by, he said, "Look, the Lamb of God!" (John 1:35-36).*

John the Baptist called Jesus "the Lamb of God" knowing that He was the innocent One who would die for the guilty. He would give His life to absorb our death penalty.

JTB is a great model for me. He understood it wasn't about him. He reminds me of the little girl who had a birthday party and invited twelve friends. One of her friends gave her a box of chocolate candy. She opened her package and gave one of the chocolates to each of her friends, then closed the box and put it away. When her mom pointed out that she hadn't taken one for herself, she blushed and whispered, "Oh! I forgot I was here."

The greatest life I can live is a life that puts others first and points others to Christ. An others-oriented life is not a sad, restricted life, it's a joyful, wide-open life. In fact, that's how you spell joy—**J**esus... **O**thers...**Y**ou.

Life Challenge: Do this twice today: Enter a room with people in it, smile and think, *Here you are!*

10
COME AND SEE

LIVE a "come and see" life.

JOHN 1:39-46

Andrew was a disciple of John the Baptist. When John called Jesus "the Lamb of God," Andrew and a friend began to tail Jesus like two detectives. Sensing He was being followed, Jesus turned and asked them point blank what they wanted. Without hesitation, they said they wanted to know where He lived. *"Come," he replied, "and you will see" (John 1:39).*

In my grade school years, my dad showed me how to line up dominoes and then push the first one over. I began to understand the idea of a chain reaction. When Jesus said, "come and see," He initiated a chain reaction of contagious aliveness. The two disciples spent the day with Him and evidently liked what they saw. Andrew hunted down his brother Peter and told him, "We've found the one we've been looking for, the Messiah." Peter, noting his brother's excitement and shining eyes, *came and saw* for himself.

The next day Jesus found another potential disciple named Phillip from the same town as Andrew and asked him to tag along, too. The dominoes were falling. Phillip called on his friend Nathanael and told

Him about Jesus of Nazareth. *"Nazareth! Can anything good come from there?" Nathanael asked. "Come and see," said Philip (John 1:46).*

A friend of mine from high school was a very gifted athlete whose whole life was wrapped up in sports. When he developed bone cancer and lost a leg, his life took a nosedive. He became bitter, angry, hopeless—and even dangerous. One day he was reading the local newspaper and saw a picture of a girl with an inexplicable light in her eyes that riveted his attention. He said to himself, *I'm going to find out what makes a person's eyes shine like that.* He actually located the girl and found out that she was a Christ-follower. After some research, my friend decided to follow Jesus as well. Before this girl ever said a word, her eyes said, "Come and see." And that's what my friend did.

You too can live a "come and see" life. You don't have to be a theologian to point people to Jesus. You don't have to be an arm-wrestler who likes to argue. Just say, "Come and see."

Life Challenge: Ask God to let His aliveness shine in your eyes today. Ask the Holy Spirit to remind you three times today to "lighten up."

11

BI-FOCAL GOD

GOD SEES YOU through the lens of your potential in Christ.

JOHN 1:42

There is a now-familiar gesture where a person points to himself, then points two fingers at his own eyes, and then points to another person. That little hand motion clearly means, *I'm watching you!* Jesus may have made that gesture when Andrew brought his brother, Simon Peter, to Him.

> *And he brought him to Jesus. Jesus looked at him and said, "You are Simon son of John. You will be called Cephas" (which, when translated, is Peter)(John 1:42).*

Jesus told Peter, "I'm watching you." When Jesus looks at you, He doesn't just look *at you*, He looks *into you*. Jesus knew Peter, understood all his faults, and yet also knew his potential more than anyone else. After that quick encounter, He gave Peter a new name that was much more than a nickname. In that culture at that time, your name represented your lineage and your character. Jesus called Simon "Rocky."

(Peter means rock). He saw something foundational in Peter that others hadn't seen.

When Jesus looks into us, He sees it all—our potential, our flaws, the whole nine yards. A few years after He first met Peter, Jesus told His disciples they would all abandon Him. Peter said, "I won't ever abandon you. I will stay with you through thick and thin, dead or alive." Jesus then informed Peter that he would deny even knowing his Lord repeatedly that very night. Jesus isn't blind to the negative things in us. He's bifocal. He sees us both as we are and as we could be.

Like Peter, you and I were designed with our potential aliveness in mind. The best thing we can do to increase our aliveness is to get close to the one who sees who we are and who we are meant to be. *My frame was not hidden from you when I was made…when I was woven together…. Your eyes saw my unformed body. All the days ordained for me were written in your book before one of them came to be"(Psalm 139:15-16).*

Life Action: Ask God to tell you one thing He sees in you today. Listen all day for His answer.

12

HOW DO YOU KNOW ME?

GOD KNOWS you completely.

JOHN 1:43-51

When my son Jeremy was eleven, I took him archery hunting. I called in a monster bull elk and it stopped only twenty yards from him. "Dad," my little hunter told me later, "I was *scared!* I was hiding in one of those little fir trees. I could almost feel his breath, but he didn't see me."

In today's reading, a man named Nathanael was snuggled under a fig tree when his friend Phillip came to take him to meet Jesus. Meeting Nathaniel, Jesus promptly declared things about this stranger that sounded like He had known him all his life.

> *"How do you know me?' Nathanael asked. Jesus answered, "I saw you while you were still under the fig tree before Philip called you" (John 1:48).*

Long before Google Earth could have helped Him zoom in on a fig tree in Israel, the Spirit revealed to Jesus not only Nathanael's location, but his inner condition, his very character.

Jesus Christ knows us because He made us. Scripture tells us that all things, including people, including you and me, were made for Him and through Him (see Romans 11:36). *Through him all things were made; without him nothing was made that has been made (John 1:3).*

When God made us, He created within us a desire to be known. That desire to be seen and acknowledged by others is a big part of our relational nature.

And God certainly knows us! He knows who we really are behind all of our masks and disguises. Jesus gave Peter new news about Peter (verse 42), and then told Nathanael supposedly private things about Nathaniel (verse 48). Over and over, Jesus told people unknown things about their character and potential, secrets about the very essence of who they were meant to be and could be.

Since God knows me even better than I know myself, perhaps I should ask Him what He knows. Once I catch a glimpse of what God sees in me, I'll never be the same.

Life Challenge: First find a watch or clock. Then ask God if there is anything He knows about you that He wants you to know also. Still your mind and listen to His voice for at least one minute.

13
NOT YET

GOD'S TIMING is always perfect.

John 2:1-4

I was born almost two months premature. When my dad first saw me—all skin and bones—he smiled, shook his head, and said to the nurse, "Put him back in. He's not done yet!"

I showed up too early, a habit I've maintained throughout my whole life.

The apostle John chose seven different miracles, seven signs of life, as the framework for his book. The first sign was when Jesus turned water into wine. It was a stunning miracle but, in one sense, it might have been almost too early.

At this point, Jesus had already chosen four or five disciples and was in the blocks waiting for the starting gun of His public ministry to sound. At the wedding in Bethany, His mother asked Him to do something special to resupply a ceremony that had run out of wine. Weddings without wine didn't work in that culture. In fact, a wedding without wine was legal grounds for suing the groom's parents. When Mary asked her son Jesus to step into that situation, He replied, *"Dear woman, why do you involve me? ...My time has not yet come"* (John 2:4).

Jesus didn't just snap His fingers and perform a miracle whenever He wanted. Later in His ministry, He said, "I do only what I see the Father doing." What's more, He acted only when He saw the Father acting. Jesus mentioned the importance of correct timing over and over in His three years of public ministry. Too many miracles too soon would mean He would be killed before God's designated time.

Timing is critical in life. It's important in pregnancy, birth, poetry, sports, cooking, joke-telling, and skydiving. Timing is important to God, too, and it's an element He uses to fine-tune our obedience.

I wonder what Mary would have done if, at the wedding in Cana, the Lord had said, "Not now" or "Not yet"? We'll never know because Jesus, receiving the green light from heaven, went ahead and made a large quantity of miracle wine.

"Not yet" isn't easy for me. Everything in me wants to run ahead, arrive early, beat the clock, and finish the task before I've even found out what it involves. How about you? If you missed the mark, would it tend to be too late or too early? One important thing about being a student-follower of Jesus is getting synchronized with God and His Holy Spirit. Are you? In one of his letters, the apostle Paul wrote these wise words: *Since we live by the Spirit, let us keep in step with the Spirit (Galatians 5:25).*

Life Challenge: Write down one thing you anticipate and look forward to. How difficult would it be for you to hear God say, "Not yet" to that plan or event?

14

DO WHATEVER HE TELLS YOU

OBEDIENCE is miracle-fuel.

John 2:5-8

In the Jewish culture of New Testament days, weddings were important week-long celebrations, filled with joy and laughter, food and wine. The groom's family was usually responsible for providing the wine—and yes, it was a very big deal.

Jesus, His mother and a few of His disciples were at a wedding in Bethany when the wine supply ran out. The Lord's mother decided to intervene, perhaps because she was a close friend of the bridegroom's family. She went to the servants and gave them some wise advice regarding her Son: *"Do whatever he tells you" (John 2:5).*

And that's what they did. When He directed them to fill six huge stone jars with water, *they filled them to the brim (John 2:7).* After that, Jesus told them to dip some water out of the jars and take it to the master of the banquet. Again, they did exactly as He said…and an amazing thing happened. The master of the banquet sniffed and sipped the freshly-drawn well water turned to wine, and was stunned by the delicious aroma and balanced, harmonious flavor.

Jesus saved someone's reputation and made for a merrier wedding.

Beyond that, He showed that miracles are often primed with acts of obedience. Obeying Him twice, the servants filled the jars to the brim with water and took the liquid to the master of the wedding. They obeyed the word of the Lord, even when it made no sense to them.

So it was with most of the miracles Jesus presided over. He said words like *"Look at Me." "Come here." "Seat the people." "Go dip in the pool." "Take up your mat."* God's power is 99 percent of any miracle, but my obedience is usually the other one percent.

Without Him, I can't.

Without me, He won't.

Life Action: Write this on a piece of paper and put it on your bedside stand or tape it to your bathroom mirror: *Do whatever He tells you.* Tonight, before you go to bed, try to think of one time when you heard His voice and obeyed "to the brim."

15
WATER TO WINE

DON'T just look AT a miracle, look INTO a miracle.

John 2:9-11

The apostle John built the first half of his gospel around seven miraculous signs that Jesus performed. Each of these signs points *beyond* the meeting of a temporal human need to something even deeper, richer, and more permanent. Each of these signs points to the unstoppable aliveness of God, available in His eternal Son, Jesus Christ.

The Lord's first recorded miracle, changing water to wine, was a supernatural sign pointing to what His life on earth would accomplish. First, the six water jugs, used for ritual washing in the Jewish religion, represent our religious attempts to clean up our outer, visible lives. (Six is the number of mankind in the Bible).

Second, the servant's obedience to the Lord's command represents what happens when any person trusts God for her or his salvation.

Third, the water made wine represents the blood of Jesus that would be shed on the cross, just as it does today when Christians participate in communion.

Fourth, the manager of the feast represents Father God, who will officiate at the wedding of Jesus and His bride, the church.

Fifth, the master's approval of the wine represents God's approval of Christ's work of atonement. *…And the master of the banquet tasted the water that had been turned into wine (John 2:9). Then he called the bridegroom aside and said, "Everyone brings out the choice wine first and then the cheaper wine after the guests have had too much to drink; but you have saved the best till now." (John 2:9b-10)* This Galilean wedding miracle was a sign, pointing to God's plan of salvation and the wedding feast of the Lamb.

What else can we learn from this first miracle, this sign? Maybe we could put it like this: Don't give God a glass of lukewarm water at the final wedding feast on that final day. Don't find yourself saying, "I really tried to clean up my life. I hope I lived a good enough life to please You." Count on it, the Father will expect good wine. It would have been better to say "I know that I didn't live up to Your standards, God. I'm not here on the basis of my righteousness or religious works. I believe in Jesus and His death for me on the cross. I believe in the blood represented by the wine I drink when I participate in holy communion. I saw the sign, and I understood it."

Life Question: Think on this for 60 seconds, or until you can formulate an answer: Why would Jesus launch His ministry with a miracle that previewed His whole plan for saving people?

16

HIS DISCIPLES PUT THEIR FAITH IN HIM

BELIEVE into Jesus.

John 2:11

When Jesus turned the water into wine, He met a felt need and previewed His entire mission. Yes, He got the steward of the wedding feast out of an embarrassing jam, but His miracle did more than that. It extended an invitation to connect personally with His unending aliveness.

Water to wine. Is that believable? I love the story of the abusive alcoholic father who surrendered his life to Christ. From that day forward, everything in his life changed. He even started reading his Bible at work during lunch. One day when a scoffer asked him what he was reading, the man replied, "I'm reading the Bible story where Jesus turned water into wine." The critic laughed and said, "You don't believe that fairytale, do you?" The converted man looked up from his Bible with a smile. "Sure I do," he said. "After all, He turned beer into new furniture at my house."

Seeing His wedding miracle, Jesus' disciples began to believe in and connect with His glorious aliveness. *This, the first of his miraculous signs,*

Jesus performed at Cana in Galilee. He thus revealed his glory, and his disciples put their faith in him (John 2:11).

So many people think that "putting faith in Jesus" or "believing in Jesus" simply means giving intellectual assent to the fact that He is God's Son. The Bible, however, teaches us that even demons believe in God—and it does them no good at all! (James 2:9). Let me try to explain the difference between believing *in* Jesus and believing *into* Jesus.

Evel Knievel was a daredevil entertainer who attempted 75 ramp-to-ramp motorcycle jumps between 1965 and 1980. In 1975, his longest jump cleared fourteen large buses in Kings Island, Ohio. Imagine for a moment if you had been there for that jump over the buses. Imagine Evel asking those who believed he could make that massive leap to raise their hands. In response, you raise your hand because you "believe in" Evel. But then what if he asked you to climb on the back of his motorcycle and ride behind him as he jumped. That would be a different proposition, isn't it? Riding with him would be "believing into" Evel.

In the same way, believing *into* Christ is betting your life on Him. That's the kind of belief that enables you to literally connect with His life. John chronicled Christ's life and His miracles so that you and I *"might believe and have life…" (John 20:31).*

In other words, get on the back of His motorcycle. You're in for the ride of your life.

Life Action: "Believing into" is not a once-for-all thing so much as a repeated day-by-day choice we make. With each new morning, we keep receiving Jesus. Picture one thing you can do today to "get on His motorcycle."

17

GIVE OR TAKE?

A LIFE-giving Church.

JOHN 2:12-16

There are millions of de-churched people in America, former church-go-ers who no longer show up on Sundays. Some are upset with a particular church or pastor, while others are apathetic or disgusted toward churches in general.

Did you know Jesus got upset with church? He went to the temple (the church of His day) and became so incensed by what He saw that He started overturning tables. Making a whip of ropes, Jesus lashed out at sacred cows and shut down Costco-church.

The Message paraphrase says He *upended the tables of the loan sharks (John 2:15, MSG)* What were sharks doing in church? They were doing what sharks just naturally do: looking for someone to chomp on. They're takers; life-takers. I wonder if one of the saddest sights on the planet in God's eyes is when church gatherings that were meant to give people life actually begin to chomp life out of people.

Have you ever caught yourself in a church service thinking about what people could do for you rather than what you could do for people? Maybe it wasn't you catching yourself, but God's Holy Spirit catching you. We can be glad that He convicts us when we let our thoughts drift in those self-centered directions.

Jesus wasn't that way at all; He was, and is, the perfect minister. One day when He went to the synagogue, He stood up and read His mission statement from the scriptures. And yes, it was all about Him…about Him giving freedom, about Him giving hope, and Him giving relief and life. (Luke 4:18-21)

Jesus hates life-depleting situations and institutions. He wants churches to be life-giving, not life-taking, places. I'm happy to say that the church I attend has set a ten-year goal of giving away ten times as much as we do now.

It makes me nervous (and a little bit angry) when church leaders make long, emotional appeals before taking up the offering. Sure, giving is proof of love, and you can't separate finances and faith. But when the top of a preacher's head starts looking like a shark fin, I get a little worried.

Life Action: The next time you head for a church meeting, ask the Holy Spirit to show you two specific opportunities to give love and life to someone—then notice what God gives to you through that process.

18
LIVING PROOF

JESUS IS LIVING PROOF of unstoppable aliveness.

JOHN 2:17-22

The miraculous signs in the gospel of John point to the unending life available to those who believe *into* Jesus.

When Christ's disciples saw Him cleanse the temple, they remembered a scripture about the Messiah's passion: *Zeal for your house will consume me (John 2:17)*. Something clicked for eleven of them. A new piece of the puzzle fell into place.

Others viewed the temple cleansing from a doubtful perspective. They got pushy and demanded a special miracle to prove that Jesus had heavenly authority to do what He did. They were sign seekers, but their hardness of heart blurred their vision.

Okay, Jesus said in effect, here is your special miracle…. *"Destroy this temple and I will raise it again in three days." (John 2:19)*. I believe Jesus tapped His own chest when He said, "this temple." It makes sense, doesn't it? A temple is a place where God meets with man, and Jesus is the ultimate place where God meets with man.

The cynical, hard-hearted sign seekers incorrectly assumed He was speaking of the Jewish temple. They scoffed at what they interpreted to be His promise that if this Jewish architectural jewel, forty-six years in the making, were destroyed, He would raise it back up in three days.

But signs of life can be interpreted in more than one way. After the resurrection of Jesus, the Eleven came to understand that *the temple he had spoken of was his body (John 2:21)*. Note these three words: '*Then they believed…*' *(John 2:22)*. Some signs of life make sense when we first see them. Others must be noted, remembered and understood later. Have you ever heard God say something to you that didn't make sense when you first heard it, but you just held onto His word, and had those very words eventually become faith-building proof of His authenticity and aliveness?

Is God the source of deep, unending aliveness? Can I connect with God through Christ and experience, now and forever, that aliveness? Yes; and yes. Jesus, who promised to share His eternal vitality with those who believed in Him, is living proof of the availability of God's amazing, unstoppable aliveness.

Life Action: Think of one thing God said to you that doesn't make sense…yet. Promise Him you will hold onto that word until He explains something further to you about it or until it comes to pass.

19

HELP MY UNBELIEF

BE HONEST WITH GOD about your unbelief.

JOHN 2:23-25

My parents took me water skiing for the first time when I was eight. I received some basic instructions, but no one bothered to tell me that when you fall, you're supposed to *let go of the rope.* As a result, when I took my first tumble, I held on for all I was worth, making myself into a human torpedo behind the boat until it finally stopped.

Ten years later, I found myself holding on for dear life again. This time, I was holding on spiritually as a new Christian clinging to God's Word. At times I found myself wondering if the Bible was real—or even if God was real. Lacking faith, I considered letting go of my rope to new hope.

In one such moment of doubt I remember sitting in my bedroom saying, "Dear God, I'm full of doubt and disbelief. I pretty much feel like You don't exist, but—I wish You did! If You are there and You do hear me, I want to go on record with You. I present my life to you one hundred percent, and only ask one thing of You. *Just let me know You are real.*"

For the next six months, I wavered between belief and unbelief.

However, as I continued to read the Bible and hold onto God's Word, He revealed to me signs of His existence and His life. My faith slowly grew stronger. Like a new skier who experiences the exhilaration of staying up, I experienced the rush and joy of His aliveness deep within me.

Toward the end of John's gospel, we read: *Now while he was in Jerusalem at the Passover Feast, many people saw the miraculous signs he was doing and believed in his name. But Jesus would not entrust himself to them, for he knew all men (John 20:23-25).* Like those people in Jerusalem at the feast, I had very little faith in those days, and the Lord knew that. He knew me from the inside out.

I can't tell you how glad I am for resolving to hang onto that rope! Over the last several decades, I've had some down times, but my faith has grown stronger month by month and year by year. Yes, I have a long, long way to go. I often find myself saying to Christ what a man with a demon-possessed son said to Him, 'I do believe, please help me overcome unbelief.' He will do that for us. I've found that God is quick to respond to sincere pleas for stronger faith.

Life Question: Think of one area in your life where you can say to the Lord, "Please help my unbelief." Do it. He loves that prayer and He will answer.

20
SURPRISED BY LIFE

LIFE IS NOT FULL…if it has no surprises.

John 3:1-7

Over and over in the gospel of John, we see that miracles are signposts pointing to the life available in Jesus Christ. In John 3:2, we see another reference to miraculous signs.

In essence, Jesus said to the Jewish religious leader Nicodemus, 'You saw some miracles, but you missed the signs. A person needs new eyes to see into the arena where God operates, and these new eyes come with a second birth, a personal regeneration.'

Jesus spoke about a whole new level of life—a spiritual, eternal level superseding the biological. Second birth gives people spiritual senses allowing them to perceive beyond what they experience through their physical senses.

To help Nicodemus understand, Jesus used the metaphor of wind. The spiritual life, He told Him, might be compared to a windy night. You can't see the wind, but you know very well that it's there. How do you know? Because you can *hear* it and *feel* it. To discern the presence of wind, then, you have to switch from sight, to sound, to feeling. In a similar way, to understand and experience Jesus' miracles, you must use your "second-birth senses."

When Nicodemus still didn't get it, he asked Jesus: "How can this be?" and Jesus said, 'I've explained these invisible, spiritual truths to you using earthy metaphors, and you still don't get it! And you're a spiritual leader and teacher of God's people! How could that be?' Back at the beginning of the conversation, the Lord noted that Nicodemus had been *surprised* by His words. He said, *"You should not be surprised at my saying, 'You must be born again'" (John 3:7).*

In this man's case, surprise was a good sign. In the original Greek, we read that the Lord's words were *a wonder* to him. When you are surprised your eyes open wide. For a moment, you hold yourself stock-still. You ask yourself, *Am I seeing this right? Am I hearing this right? Could this really be?* Nicodemus was surprised on his way to awareness. Later in the Bible, we discover that he became a Christ-follower.

In our walk with Jesus as well, surprise sometimes comes before comprehension. You see something in the Word or hear something taught in church and it stops you in your tracks. You say, "Could this be true? Could this really work for me?" We call surprises like that *fresh revelation*, and we all need it.

Life Question: When was the last time God stopped you in your tracks with a truth that touched your life in a new way?

21
GET THE POINT?

YOU can be a living miracle.

JOHN 3:3-11

Nicodemus was beginning to believe that Jesus, whom he respectfully called "Rabbi," might be able to teach him something new. *"Rabbi, we all know you're a teacher straight from God. No one could do all the God-pointing, God-revealing acts you do if God weren't in on it" (John 3:2, MSG).*

I have two pointing dogs, a German Shorthair and a German Wirehair. When we are on a rocky hillside and one of them instantly freezes, nose forward, tail straight up, I get the point. I hate to admit it, but at times I may be more alert to bird-pointing acts than to God-pointing acts.

I like how The Message translation calls Jesus' miracles "God-pointing acts." Jesus told Nicodemus that he had not been seeing where those acts were pointed. *"Take it from me: Unless a person is born from above, it's not possible to see what I'm pointing to—to God's kingdom" (John 3:3, MSG).*

Nicodemus may not have understood it at the time, but he was under conviction by God's Holy Spirit. He knew that Jesus was talking about something he didn't have—and that receiving the God-life Jesus offered would require him to do something very radical and become someone very different. God-life was something that could not be learned in college or earned by obtaining another diploma. He didn't need more information or more education. What he needed, to put it simply, was to be born a second time, born into the realm where God is Lord and King.

All of a sudden Nic's collar felt too tight, and beads of sweat began to form on his forehead. The angels were singing "Just As I Am," and Nicodemus didn't want to go to the altar—or not yet, at least. He really didn't want to grapple with the reality right in front of his eyes because of where he knew that truth would lead. For Nicodemus, secure in his position, status, and reputation, it would mean doing something and becoming someone radical and unfamiliar. Life as he had known it would completely change.

> *Jesus said, "You're a respected teacher of Israel and you don't know these basics? Listen carefully. I'm speaking sober truth to you. I speak only of what I know by experience; I give witness only to what I have seen with my own eyes. There is nothing secondhand here, no hearsay. Yet instead of facing the evidence and accepting it, you procrastinate with questions" (John 3:10-11, MSG).*

What's the point? It's one thing to see a miracle, but it's another thing to *become* a miracle…by kneeling down, asking forgiveness, receiving Jesus, and being born into His forever family.

Life Challenge: Next time the wind is blowing, stand outside for a minute and thank God for the presence and the voice of His Holy Spirit.

22

ANTIDOTE FOR DEATH

DEFEAT DEATH by coming to the cross and looking up.

JOHN 3:12-15

I've loved the outdoors my whole life, but I have never been fond of snakes. When I encounter a rattlesnake out in the wild country, I keep a respectful distance. My wife's uncle Charlie was bitten by a rattler while fishing the Malheur River in Oregon. His organs began to shut down, and organ failure eventually took his life.

Jesus Christ said He came *down* from heaven to be lifted *up* on a cross, just as Moses lifted up a snake in the desert. (John 3:13-14). The snake-bite story is found in Numbers 21:1-9. Plagued with poison vipers, Israelites were dying by the boatload. When Moses asked God how to stop the curse, God told him to make a copper snake and affix it to a tall pole. God said, *"whoever is bitten and looks at it will live."* Snake-bitten people who gazed at the serpent on a pole were saved from a painful death.

On the cross, Jesus was lifted up like that copper serpent. The Bible says He *became sin* for us. Jesus became a snake and a savior at the same time. God the Father looked away from His Son as Jesus absorbed our sin and came to represent the iniquity of the whole world for all time. He took our poison and died in our place.

Many years ago, I became convinced I was poisoned inside—destined for death unless I found an antidote. I came to the cross of Christ and looked up. There I saw the One who offered Himself to the fangs of death so I could live. *"… The Son of Man must be lifted up, that everyone who believes in him may have eternal life" (John 3:14-15).*

That's how God saves people. He invites them simply to come to the cross and look up. I'm so glad I did that. It changed my eternal address and gave me a whole new start on a whole new life. That moment before the cross literally transformed me from the inside out and continues to shape and reshape me to this very day. Day by day, as I look up, His death becomes my life.

Life Action: Can you remember what you were like before you came to the cross and looked up? Thank God for taking the poison that was intended for you.

23
SAVED FROM...

THE OLD ME is terminal.

JOHN 3:16

Jesus talked a lot about taking up our cross and dying to self. Life in Christ is not a matter of *turning over a new leaf*, it is a matter of *receiving a new life*. On the cross, Jesus refused to save Himself although He had the power to do it. He knew that if He saved Himself, He couldn't have saved you and me.

I grew up in an evangelical Christian family and heard the word "saved" a lot. *Jesus saves*. What does that mean? It means that Jesus gives us a ticket to heaven—and a whole lot more. When we say that Jesus saves us, it means that He repairs and restores us. He helps us, forgives us, redeems us, and frees us to live the life we were created to live.

A few years after I became a Christ-follower, I joined with some other young adults offering a free car wash in our city on a Saturday. People would drive in and ask, "What's the catch?" And we would say, "No catch. We just want to demonstrate God's love." People seemed to appreciate the free wash.

I remember opening the car door for a guy whose car had just been washed and hearing one of the zealous young people washing cars call out to him, "Jesus saves!" The guy turned to me and whispered, "Jesus saves from what?" The normal Christian answer would be "Jesus saves from sin," or "Jesus saves us from hell." Without even thinking, I said to the guy, "He saves me from myself; from being the old, selfish me." He acted surprised at my answer. He stood there silent for several moments, smiled, and then said, "I'll have to think about that."

"To save" is to deliver from a bad state to a better state. The old me, the B.C. (before Christ) me, was biologically alive but spiritually dead. Biological aliveness is very nice, but it's terminal. The old me is self-centered, selfish and terminal. The new me, the AD me, is Christ-centered, loving and non-perishable. *For God so loved the world that he gave his one and only Son, that whoever believes in him shall not perish… (John 3:16a).*

To perish is to die, but the word used here in John 3:16 also means to be rendered useless. God doesn't want you to die, but He also doesn't want you to be destroyed, to be rendered useless, to 'perish' in spite of being physically alive.

Life Action: Jesus came to save you from useless, purposeless, terminal living. Are you thankful? Tell Him right now and at least one more time today!

24

SAVED TO...

JESUS wants to save us TO something.

John 3:16

A savior is someone who delivers you from a bad state to a better state. Just before His death, when Jesus entered Jerusalem, the crowds lining the road yelled "Hosanna," which means "save us, we pray."

Save. We've shrunk the word by narrowing it to mean a pass out of hell, a ticket into heaven. And yes, God really does save us from spending eternity living at the wrong address! But He saves us not only *from* something, but *to* something.

> *For God so loved the world that he gave his one and only Son, that whoever believes in him shall not perish but have eternal life (John 3:16).*

'*...Shall not perish...*' He saves us *from* eternal death. If He is our savior, we won't perish, we won't be ruined, and we won't end up being disconnected from God forever. '*...But have eternal life.*' He saves us *to* a whole new dimension of aliveness, now and forever.

When the Israelites were saved from slavery in Egypt, they were meant to be blessed in the promised land. Sadly, all but two of them failed to make it into the land God had prepared for them. They experienced a part of their salvation but failed to experience the rest.

I'm afraid the same thing happens today. When Christ becomes our savior, He intends to save us into a new aliveness that is deeper, richer, longer and stronger. That new aliveness starts now and lasts forever.

Being saved from hell and eternal death is a gift beyond comprehension. But there is so much more! We are also saved to live a 'here-and-now-life' on earth that becomes more and more like the 'fully-alive-life' Jesus modeled. We can start living the first part of eternal life right now, 24/7.

Life Action: A strong purpose in life? Joy that bubbles up in spite of your circumstances? A new-found unselfishness? Stop tonight before you go to bed and thank God for one thing that you appreciate being "saved to" today.

25
EXPOSED

LIGHT HAS COME into the world. Get exposed!

John 3:17-21

In my early teens, some friends and I misbehaved one night. We threw a huge rotten pumpkin onto someone's porch and watched it explode. Porch lights and yard lights came on. An angry man screamed obscenities. I ran for darkness as fast as I could.

That's what you do when you know you've done wrong. You run for the darkness. John's gospel says, *God's light came into the world, but people loved the darkness more than the light, for their actions were evil (John 3:19, NLT).*

Jesus is God-light—that bright, pure, resplendent revelation of Himself. As I approach Jesus, that blazing radiance reveals truth about God—and truth about me, too. Many times, I don't like what I see about me when I come into the light. The Message translation of John 3:20 says that we fail to move toward God-light because we fear **"a painful exposure."**

I've learned first-hand that the closer I get to Christ, the more my sins and shortcomings are exposed. I become progressively aware of the remaining areas of darkness in myself.

But, thank God, if I confess my sin—all those stinky, messy, rotten pumpkin bombs—God forgives my sins and helps me clean the porch. But if I make excuses or run from the light, those sins will be painfully exposed on the Day of Judgment. To sum up, then, I judge myself by how I respond to the light.

> *"God sent his Son into the world not to judge the world,*
> *but to save the world through him" (John 3:17, NLT).*

God tells us, through John, why He sent Jesus to planet earth. He did it to connect people to Him and His aliveness. The message of the Bible is not "God is ticked" but "God is love." Jesus came into the world to be a savior, not a fault-finder, a lighthouse, not a spotlight.

Let's be truth-tellers, confession-makers, and light-lovers!

Life Challenge: Ask God to make you a light-lover, even if it means you'll become more aware of the sins He sees in your life.

26

MAIN ATTRACTION

REMINDER TO SELF: It's not about me.

JOHN 3:22-30

I remember watching a cowboy movie where one cowboy said to the other, "There ain't enough room in this town for both of us. It's too crowded." He patted his revolver and said, "One way or another, one of us is gonna be gone by sundown."

When John the Baptist and his apprentices were baptizing people in the Jordan River, they became a national attraction, with people coming from far and wide to be baptized. Then Jesus and His disciples began to do the same, not far away. Soon after, the tide began to shift. An increasing percentage of people desiring to be baptized were now going to the Jesus group.

Feeling belittled, John's disciples got edgy. They came to John for moral support, bemoaning the fact that they were playing second fiddle to Jesus. John told his disciples that what was happening was good because he wasn't the main attraction, Jesus was (John 3:29).

This book points out the signs of life in John's gospel. John the Baptist was certainly one of those signposts. When you think about it, a directional sign doesn't invite people to come to the sign itself, it invites people to come to someone/someplace other than itself. John was overjoyed that people were going to where, and to Whom, His life pointed.

If I want to be a sign of life, I have to remember the first four words in Rick Warren's popular book *Purpose Driven Life:* "It's not about you." As I've already mentioned, I went a whole year saying that to myself at least once a day.

People helpers, including Christian leaders, make a mistake when they teach people to constantly come to them and depend on them, rather than teaching them to take their questions, needs, and requests directly to God. We should beware of "needing to be needed."

When my German shorthair goes on point ten feet from a pheasant hiding in the brush, it's a beautiful thing. I admire the dog, yes, but quickly shift my attention to where she is pointing. The bird! That's the main attraction.

Life Question: Would someone watching a "dawn to dark" video of your life yesterday think you were the main attraction, or that the Lord was?

27
HEAVEN-BORN LIFE

HEAVEN-BORN LIFE is complete and forever.

JOHN 3:31-36

The two main Greek words for "life" in the New Testament are *bios* (biological life) and *zoe* (spiritual life). *Bios* is earthborn, terminal aliveness, while *zoe* is heaven-born, eternal aliveness. Jesus taught about *zoe* life—and knew better than anyone who has ever left footprints on this earth what He was talking about. *"The One who comes from above is head and shoulders over other messengers from God... the heaven-born is in a league of his own" (John 3:31, MSG).*

Jesus used the term "born from above" when He was talking to Nicodemus (John 3:3, msg). In Romans 8:29 (NLT) Christ is called **the first-born among many brothers and sisters.** He is the first of many heaven-born daughters and sons. When a person is born again, born from above, he or she is born into a new kind of life. Deep, unending *zoe* life.

The purpose of John's gospel is to help people believe in Jesus as the giver of eternal life. Jesus used a courtroom metaphor when He said that He Himself *"...sets out the evidence of what he saw and heard in heaven" (John 3:33a, MSG).*

For years, scientists have been looking for signs of life on Mars—and now their search has broadened deeper and deeper into the galaxy. The biggest sign of life anyone could ever find, however, is Jesus Christ. All the other signs of life point to Him, the source of *zoe* life.

> *"That is why whoever accepts and trusts the Son gets in on everything, life complete and forever! And that is also why the person who avoids and distrusts the Son is in the dark and doesn't see life. All he experiences of God is darkness, and an angry darkness at that"* (John 3:36, MSG).

If Christ is who He says He is, if He is eternal aliveness, then to be disconnected from Him is to be destined for darkness and death. Choosing to reject Jesus is a deliberate decision to reject both light and life. Do you want to see eternal life and the bright splendor of heaven? It all starts with seeing Jesus for who He is, and then reaching out to Him in simple faith.

Life Challenge: Commit to higher education. Alone with Him, ask Him out loud to be your class professor and to teach you more every day about *zoe* life.

28

THE GIFT OF GOD

BE A DISTRIBUTOR of free life in Jesus.

JOHN 4:1-10

Jesus was led by the Spirit to take the unorthodox route from Judea to Galilee. I believe *"he had to go through Samaria" (John 4:4, NLT)* because He had a gift to deliver to a person He'd never met.

On the way to Galilee via Samaria Jesus and the disciples came to a well, and Jesus waited there as His followers went into town to buy food. (It takes 12 grown men to buy food? Maybe it was because the Samaritans would have no dealings with Jews, so it was hard to find an available store.) John tells us that Jesus was tired from the long, dusty journey. Amazing! Jesus the Christ, pure eternal energy, cloaked Himself in an earth-suit and became susceptible to weariness.

After a time, Jesus lifted His eyes and saw the one He had come so far to meet, a Samaritan woman on her way to draw water at the well. In the moments that followed, Jesus used a question to draw her into a life-changing conversation. "Will you give Me a drink?" He asked.

She stopped in her tracks. "Wow. Where's Your Jewish prejudice? How can You associate with me, a woman and a Samarian, and ask me for a drink?"

Jesus answered her, "If you knew the gift of God and who it is that asks you for a drink, you would have asked him, and he would have given you living water" (John 4:10). As the conversation continued, Jesus offered—and she accepted—the gift of God-aliveness. Deep, lasting, thoroughly satisfying LIFE.

These verses are packed with lessons for would-be distributors of God-aliveness:

Sharing life starts with following the Spirit's lead *("he had to go")*. Sharing life often happens while I'm "on the way" to somewhere else *(Galilee)*. Sharing life begins with association *(How can you associate with me?)*. Sharing life starts with finding a common interest or need *(Cool water on a hot day)*. Sharing life is ultimately about a Person and not a religion *(Jesus)*.

Life Action: Find a common interest with one person you've never met and ask a question about that shared interest. See where it leads.

29
LIVING WELL

TWO KINDS OF WATER give two kinds of life.

JOHN 4:11-14

I read about a study funded by the Department of Health and Human Services a few years ago. A panel of experts in psychology and economics gathered to try to define a reliable measure of human well-being.

When you ask a person, "How are you?" a common answer is, "I'm doing well, thank you." Their *'well'* is an adverb, but *a well* is also a noun, a place of life-giving water.

Jesus had a divine appointment with a woman at a well in a little city called Sychar. She made her way to that village water source late on what was probably a hot morning. The well was deep, and drawing the water took effort. With so many ex-husbands she was probably a social outcast, and wouldn't have come to the well early when the respectable women were there.

Jesus asked her for a drink of water, the kind of water that enables biological (terminal) life. He reminded her that she had to come to this well over and over and told her that a special kind of water was available from Him, water that would quench her thirst for aliveness, right then and forever.

*"Whoever drinks the water I give him will never thirst.
Indeed, the water I give him will become in him a spring
of water welling up to eternal life" (John 4:14).*

"Never thirst." Sounds appealing, doesn't it? So where do you and I go to pull on a rope and draw up a bucketful of aliveness? There are so many kinds of wells. Banks. Offices. Factories. Entertainment. Recreation. Relationships. Approval. Sex. Food. Drink. Each of these things quenches some kind of thirst, and each of them is temporary.

Christ spoke of an artesian life-spring, where water simply bubbles up from deep places and continuously overflows. What a great picture of perpetual satisfaction, of having something deep inside that is so alive it pushes its way to the surface.

Life Challenge: When someone asks you today, "How are you?" say "I'm well. In fact, I'm an artesian well." If they ask you what you mean, take a minute to tell them about John 4:11-14.

30
SPEAKING OF THIRST

JESUS KNOWS US…and loves us still.

JOHN 4:15-18

The woman who met Jesus at the well in Sychar was thirsty. Biologically, she was thirsty for water. She was also thirsty for fulfillment, satisfaction, love, and life.

> *The woman said to him, "Sir, give me this water so that I won't get thirsty and have to keep coming here to draw water" (John 4:15).*

Thinking about her thirst for life, Jesus said, "Go get your husband." She said, "I have no husband." "That's true," Jesus replied, "You've had five husbands and you're now living with a man-friend." He knew that each of her marriages had been a leaky cistern. Each of her relationships was like drinking salt-water. Instead of satisfying her deepest thirst for life, it dehydrated her spiritually—to the point that she was now desperately thirsty.

The human race is a thirsty bunch. Thirst for life is a desire that the Creator put into all of His creatures. Why? Why aren't we satisfied with simple survival? Why aren't we content with mere existence? I believe God made us thirsty to draw us to Him. Jesus Christ is both the thirst-giver and the thirst-quencher. He is life-giving water to our inner deserts, and the antidote for eternal loneliness.

God made us thirsty for life and for love. Like you and me, the woman at the well had a deep-down desire to know and be known. At the same time, however, she was also *afraid* of being known. Maybe she'd been divorced by each of her five husbands. Maybe she felt that anyone who really knew her would see her flaws and write her off.

But now she is being known by Jesus, who knows very well that she's been looking for life and love in all the wrong places. To her great surprise, however, she senses no judgment. She's beginning to be loved with the God-kind-of-love. Part of being fully alive is being known by God, warts and all, and being loved anyway.

Life Action: List three things you are thirsty for. Now write one sentence that describes what you think Jesus would say to you about those three things.

31
I CAN SEE

FIND OUT MORE about who I AM is.

JOHN 4:19-26

The Bible says that all things were created by Christ and find their purpose in Him. This Samaritan woman didn't see Jesus as Creator yet, but she did see Him as a man sent by God. And that's a start. *"Sir," the woman said, "I can see that you are a prophet" (John 4:19).*

This thirsty lady began to perceive signs of life that pointed to Jesus and who He was began to dawn on her. People receive different amounts of revelation light, and each of us will be judged according to the light that we have encountered.

The woman said, "I know that Messiah (called Christ) is coming. When he comes, he will explain everything to us." Then Jesus declared, "I, who speak to you am he" (John 4:25-26). Feeling exposed by Jesus' prophetic searchlight, the woman turned the conversation to religious controversy. Jesus blocked her detour and turned the conversation back toward her thirst for a better life.

The gospel of John quotes Jesus as making many amazing "I am" claims. Here he said, '*I am* the Messiah that you have been hoping for.' And in that moment, the woman began to understand who He was.

Proverbs tells us that *understanding is a fountain of life to the one who has it (16:22, NASB)*. Understanding the identity of Jesus is a well of aliveness, the key to living better and living forever.

Years ago, a young man from India tried to convince me that his Indian guru was a Christ-man. He said, "The Spirit of Christ that was on Jesus is also on my Maharaja." I invited him to go to church with me and promised to reciprocate and go with him if he so desired. Surprisingly, he went to church, and declaring boldly that there are many different paths to God, he marched to the front row.

Sitting in the front row, in the middle of the worship service, he spun around and fell to the floor back first. God pinned him there. He was terrified. The service stopped, and people thought he'd had a heart attack. Finally, ushers pried him off the floor. When we talked after the service, it was obvious that he would be taking another look at just who Jesus is.

Jesus is still introducing people to life, to Himself. It's wonderful when you realize, as the Samaritan woman did, that you are face to face with "I AM."

Life Action: Close your eyes for 60 seconds, then open them and note the first four colors you see. Thank God for physical sight and spiritual sight.

32
THAT'S LIFE

JESUS MOVES Toward the broken places in me.

JOHN 5:1-15

While attending an annual feast in Jerusalem, Jesus made His way to the pool of Bethesda, a gathering place for people with serious handicaps. Blind people tapped their way to the pool with their canes. Crippled people came on crutches. Paralyzed people on stretchers were carried there by friends who left them at the pool.

One who was there had been an invalid for thirty-eight years. (John 5:5). As I read that verse today, the word *invalid* jumped out at me. To be an invalid means to be unsound, infirm, *unacceptable.*

I can relate to feeling unacceptable. Several years ago, I loaned the majority of our retirement money to a friend, a successful businessman who developed property. When the so-called "great recession" hit, I lost all of what I had loaned him. I felt like a financial and emotional invalid, but that's not the end of the story.

Jesus asked the debilitated man: *"Do you want to get well?" (John 5:6).* Setbacks can become excuses for not getting better and handicaps can become crutches we're afraid to live without. New opportunities, however, also mean new responsibilities. *Are you ready for new responsibility?* The way you answer that question is crucial.

In so many words, the man by the pool informed Jesus that healing—the gift of life at a higher level—was, for him, inaccessible. *Then Jesus said to him, "Get up! Pick up your mat and walk." At once the man was cured; he picked up his mat and walked. (John 5:8-9).* Fortunately, Jesus loves and helps people who feel unacceptable.

This story helps me realize that Jesus moves toward broken places in me. When Jesus went to Jerusalem, His compassion drew Him toward the pool of Bethesda, the melting pot for damaged people. And even though I may disqualify myself for healing through my attitudes or words, the Lord doesn't disqualify me.

When the Word of God talks to us about becoming more and more alive, we have to decide whether we will believe that and walk in it—or quietly disqualify ourselves from it and blame others for what we refuse to receive.

Life Challenge: Where is one place in your life where you've doubted that God could and would heal you? How, specifically, might you "pick up your mat and walk" today?

33
CROSSOVER

GOD IS GIVING life through Jesus.

JOHN 5:16-30

When I was playing basketball in junior high, a friend taught me a new move called a "crossover." You stop dribbling and plant both feet squarely. Your feet come down together, so you can pivot on either foot. As soon as your feet hit the floor, you step forward at a 45-degree angle with either foot to go past your opponent. Then, as you step beside or beyond the person guarding you, you can shoot or pass.

Jesus specialized in a different kind of crossover, saying, *"... Whoever hears my word and believes him who sent me has eternal life and will not be condemned; he has crossed over from death to life"* (John 5:24, NIV).

That is an eternal crossover. *"For just as the Father raises the dead and gives them life, even so the Son gives life to whom he is pleased to give it"* (John 5:21, NIV).

Both the Father and the Son are life-givers. They give life in four dimensions: Spirit-life, soul-life, body-life, and social-life. God quickens dead spirits. He revives dead souls. He raises dead bodies. He restores dead relationships.

"The Father loves the Son and includes him in every-thing he is doing. ....For in the same way that the Father raises the dead and creates life, so does the Son" (John 5:19-21, MSG).

Jesus said that the sum total of what the Father is doing through the Son is giving life. God is love. Love gave life to the first human beings. Love is still giving life.

Life Action: Name the top three "good things" in your life from the hand of God.

34
SIGN LANGUAGE

GOD IS SPEAKING to you in sign language.

JOHN 5:31-47

John's gospel proves who Jesus is. It does this by showing us what would happen in a courtroom with Jesus on trial. The words *witness* and *testify* occur often in John's gospel. In John 5 Jesus listed four witnesses which testified to His authenticity: (1) His miracles (signs); (2) John the Baptist; (3) God the Father; (4) The scriptures.

The book of John is saturated with signs of life. It recounts many miracles and other indicators that point to Jesus as the ultimate giver of life. His miracles said what He Himself said: *"Come to me to have life"* (John 5:40).

Jesus, in His own defense, also called the scriptures to the witness stand. *"You search the Scriptures because you think they give you eternal life. But the Scriptures point to me!" (John 5:39, NLT).* Signs point to something other than themselves. So do Christ's miracles—and the scriptures. God speaks in sign language.

Sign language saved my life. In my college years, I was part of a fire suppression crew that fought a huge forest fire in Okanogan, Washington. Our helicopter pilot was running low on fuel, so he dropped us off on a ridge at a spot that wasn't very flat. Three other guys got off. Then I got off, grabbed a chainsaw, and began to run uphill.

After a few steps, I looked up and saw my crewmembers motioning frantically with their hands, "Get down!" I bent over just in time. My buddies said that just before I bent at the waist, the helicopter blade was whirring dangerously close to the top of my head.

Sign language is all around us. I like to watch the agile people who convey the speaker's words to the deaf in our church with sign language. The seas and the skies speak to us in sign language. *"The heavens declare the glory of God; the skies proclaim the work of his hands" (Psalm 19:1).*

Those guys on my fire crew had been screaming at me at the top of their voices, but I couldn't hear them. Looking up and seeing them duck down and put their hands on the top of their heads—sign language for *get down*—gave me more years of life. As you might imagine, I'm very grateful to them. But I'm even more grateful for the sign language God shared with me, showing me the way to enjoy a bazillion more years of life!

Life Spark: Anticipate God speaking to you in sign language today.

35
MIRACLE LEFTOVERS

GOD MAY WANT YOU TO CHEW a little longer on what He is doing.

John 6:1-15

Jesus went with His disciples to the far side of the Sea of Galilee. Sitting on a hilltop, they saw a huge crowd of people coming their way. Jesus asked Philip if he had any ideas about how they could feed this horde of seekers. Philip replied that even if all twelve of the disciples had saved a month's wages, their savings wouldn't be enough to give one small piece of bread to everyone in the crowd.

Jesus and Philip saw the same crowd through two different paradigms. Jesus saw 15,000 possibilities. Pragmatic Philip saw 15,000 problems.

To stretch Philip's faith and to feed His followers, Jesus miraculously multiplied one small meal to feed the entire multitude. *When they had all had enough to eat, he said to his disciples, "Gather the pieces that are left over. Let nothing be wasted" (John 6:12).*

I wonder why there were leftovers. Was it because the size of the miracle didn't match the size of the crowd's appetite? Did the Lord miscalculate? Was there too much miracle? If Jesus could do a "full-meal-deal" for thousands of hungry people, why save the twelve baskets of leftovers?

Maybe God knew that the left-over miracle would be good to chew on for the next few days. Perhaps the twelve would meditate on the miracle and get the message. Certainly, most of the crowd misread the miracle—and then miscalculated God's timing. *Jesus saw that in their enthusiasm, they were about to grab him and make him king, so he slipped off and went back up the mountain to be by himself (John 6:15, MSG).*

The crowd missed the most important part of the message: Miracles are more about what God wants to do *in* me, than what God wants to do *for* me. A rightly read miracle doesn't bend God to what I want, it bends me to what God wants. Yes, it's obviously about what God wants to do around me, but even more profoundly about what God wants to do within me.

Maybe that miracle message became clear to Philip soon thereafter as he munched on a piece of day-old bread.

Life Challenge: Break a little piece of bread off of a slice and keep it in your pocket for 24 hours. Let it remind you that God wants to change the world by changing you.

36
FEAR'S HIGH TIDE

WHEN YOU ARE AFRAID, trust Him.

JOHN 6:16-21

Those who ate the miracle meal were ready to make Jesus king right then and there. Jesus, who always submitted to the Father's timing, headed for the hills, making it clear He wanted to be alone. The disciples grabbed their twelve baskets of left-over bread and took off across the Sea of Galilee without Him.

When ferocious winds began slapping the sea, the twelve, wet with sweat and spray, hit the panic button. I can relate to their fear. Tongue in cheek, I could say what Woody Allen said: "I'm not afraid of dying. I just don't want to be there when it happens."

When the disciples saw a solitary figure on the edge of darkness, walking toward them on the water, their fear exploded into panic. In just a few hours, they'd gone from a sunny, miraculous day in a meadow to a dark, terrifying night in a storm. Then, at fear's high tide, they thought they saw a ghost. That's when the ghost said to the superstitious sailors what God says over and over again in the Bible. *"Don't be afraid, I am here!" (John 6:20, NLT)*

I would like to think my faith is strong enough to evict all fear from my life. I wish I were always full of fearless faith. David said, *"When I am afraid, I will trust in you" (Psalm 56:3).* He didn't say he would never be afraid; he said he was experiencing both faith and fear. It reminds us of the man in the Bible who said to Jesus, "I believe, help my unbelief."

When the disciples recognized the water-walker as Jesus, their faith began to grow. *"Then they were willing to take Him into the boat (John 6:21)."* The best thing to do in a storm is to get Jesus in the boat. He won't force His way in, you have to invite Him. But He will come.

Why wouldn't everyone invite Jesus into their boat during a storm? One reason might be that when He comes in, He takes charge. He becomes the captain. This goes against my tendency to trust myself—to imagine that I can get control of a chaotic situation. I can think of several times in my life when it took a perfect storm to persuade me to take off the captain's hat and give it to Jesus.

Life Question: When was the last time you were in a storm? Did you invite Jesus into your boat? If so, is He still the Captain?

37
BREAD OF LIFE

WORK HARD for whole-life bread.

JOHN 6:22-42

In my childhood, I must have eaten a million peanut butter and jelly sandwiches. I love bread.

When Jesus miraculously multiplied a little lunch to feed thousands of people, He multiplied bread and fish. Some of the consumers of the miracle meal, while chewing on the fish and bread, must have thought, "Let's do this again tomorrow."

The day after the miracle, they searched for Jesus along the shorelines of the Sea of Galilee. When they found Him, He told them they were looking for the *right person*, but for the *wrong reason*. He said they were working hard for physical and temporal food, but they were missing the meal that would nourish their "lasting life."

When He spoke of working hard for the wrong kind of bread, they asked, "What kind of work could we do that would be pleasing to God?" *Jesus answered, "The work of God is this: to believe in the one he has sent"* *(John 6:29, NIV).*

A little irritated, they asked Him to prove himself by repeating the bread miracle of the day before. Some suggested that He should provide them with miracle bread every day, just as God did for forty years in Moses's time. Jesus said they were looking for a physical meal, but what they truly needed was spiritual bread from God. "Okay," they said, "Give us some of that bread." He replied, *"I am the bread of life" (John 6:35).*

The word *manna* means "What is it?" Jesus was trying to bring them to the point of seeing Him for who He was and is. The ultimate life-giving manna from God.

Some murmured, "We know His family," ... "How can He make the claim that He came down from heaven?" They missed the fact that God delivered His Bread of Life through the portal of a human womb.

God gave His Son to give us something more permanent and more satisfying than mere existence. He doesn't want us to settle for the physical things alone. Much better realities await us.

Life Challenge: Tonight, before your evening meal, thank the Lord for giving you nourishment that goes way, way beyond satisfying physical hunger. Thank Him for food that will sustain you for the next trillion years—just for starters.

38
DRAWN TO LIFE

GOD WILL SPEAK to you about life in understandable terms.

JOHN 6:43-60

Jesus told the crowd of miracle seekers that *everyone* who comes to Him is drawn by God. Those who respond to God's magnetism go through a process: listen, learn, believe and live. It starts with God; He initiates this process and makes us spiritually hungry. We choose how we will respond.

"I am the bread of life." (John 6:48) Jesus' teachings are rich with analogies, metaphors, parables, and similes. These four teaching tools take something unfamiliar to the listeners and make it understandable by comparing it to something familiar to the listeners. Here Jesus used a metaphor and compared Himself to bread. Every one of His listeners was familiar with bread, so they understood at least half of the equation. Many became curious about His words. How was this Teacher, this miracle-worker like bread—specifically the "bread of life"?

He uses the same methodology with you and me to this day. He takes lofty truths about abundant life off of the top shelf and sets them in our lap. He graciously speaks to us individually using the terms of our culture, our history, our language, and our current awareness.

I read an article recently in an archeology magazine. The author said that long ago, before archeology's modern era, some theologians and Christian leaders thought that the words of the New Testament were originally written in a special divine version of Greek—a heavenly Greek language God created just for the Bible's New Testament. But as archeology advanced, as scraps of papyrus and engravings were unearthed, it was found that the words in the New Testament were *common* Greek, the same words used in average citizen's grocery lists and personal reminders.

God is drawing us to Jesus, to Eternal Aliveness. He draws us with words we can understand, using familiar terms to explain things about aliveness that I'm only beginning to grasp. To the scientist, He says, "It's like electrons, neutrons, and quarks." To the plumber, He says, "Your life is leaking right here." To the vineyard owner, He says, "I am the grapevine and you are the branches." God draws every person in terms she or he can understand. Isn't that amazing?

Life-challenge: Listen all day for the Spirit to whisper, *"It's kind of like this…."* Stop tonight and think about whether you really heard those words and applied them to your life.

39
HARD TO SWALLOW

KEEP TRUSTING GOD, even if He doesn't do things the way you want Him to.

JOHN 6:61-71

Jesus reminded the manna-seekers that their forefathers who ate miraculous manna for forty years didn't live forever. He spoke of a different manna that would keep them alive eternally. "The living Bread that lasts forever came to earth so you could last forever."

Tragically, the listeners—perhaps even the most committed—choked on what He said. Noticing that His audience was offended, Jesus threw out something more for them to chew on. He asked how they would respond if God's action plan didn't line up with their expectations. *"What if you see the Son of Man ascend to where he was before!" (John 6:62)* "What if there is a 'first coming' *and* a 'second coming'?" "What if I leave earth and come back again later?" The idea of God doing things any other way than the way they had things lined out was very hard for them to swallow.

It can be very distasteful when God does things His way instead of our way. That's why most of the people who had eaten the prior day's miracle meal suddenly lost their appetite for Christ's teaching. There was a giant rush for the exit.

Yesterday 15,000 fans in the grandstands, and today only eleven remain—and they are acting antsy. He was a hero on Sunday, a zero on Monday.

Peter, still chewing on what Jesus said, spoke up. "We're staying Lord. We believe you are the Bread." *"You have the words of eternal life." (John 6:6)* "If we left, we'd starve to death." Judas, however, had something in his craw that he couldn't swallow. Eventually, it would kill him.

Life Concept: It's not crucial that you have all the answers, but it is crucial that, unlike Judas, you believe Jesus Christ does.

40

MURDER BY DEGREES

RECOGNIZE LIFE-GIVERS and life-takers.

JOHN 7:1-5

After this, Jesus went around in Galilee, purposely stay-ing away from Judea because the Jews there were waiting to take his life (John 7:1).

Jesus came to bring deep, unending life to the people on this planet. If God comes to earth to bring life and everyone wants *more* life, life should win by a landslide, right? Why would anyone want to take life away from Jesus—a person whose whole mission was to give life? (John 3:16) May-be it's like this: people who have become life-takers hate life-givers.

Jesus' skeptical brothers needled Him, satirically encouraging Him to go to Judea for the upcoming festival and whip up some miracles. Misreading His motives, they accused Him of lusting for worldwide popularity. *For even his own brothers did not believe in him (John 7:5).*

Jesus' brothers were making fun of Him and the religious officials were trying to find a way to murder Him. That's murder in different degrees. Many who would never shoot or strangle a person will take a smaller piece of life from them by criticizing them, gossiping about them, or speaking to them in a demeaning way—like the Lord's brothers did to Him. I had a fifth-grade basketball coach who told me I was clumsy. I still remember it, and how it deadened a little piece of my heart!

If we had been in Jesus' sandals at this point, most of us would have been bummed; perhaps we'd have bought more life insurance. But Jesus didn't miss a beat. He knew that the Father believed in Him even if His brothers didn't. He knew what mattered most.

Jesus purposely stayed away from the first-degree murderers in Judea, but He didn't stay away from His brothers, second-degree murderers. Sorry to say, sometimes those very close to us are life-takers. Parents, siblings, teachers, relatives, and Judases can be murderers. Only with the Spirit's help can we know which murderers to avoid.

Life Action: Thank God today for being a life-giver, then thank two other life-giving persons who add quality to your life.

41
LIFETIME

WAIT FOR GOD'S TIMING, even if it "kills you."

JOHN 7:6-14

The Lord's cynical, unbelieving half-brothers challenged Him to go where the action was, to the Feast of Tabernacles in Jerusalem. "Go ahead!" they told Him. "Stand on Your soapbox, preach to the crowds, shake hands, kiss babies, and strut Your stuff."

> *Therefore, Jesus told them, "The right time for me has not yet come; for you any time is right." (John 7:6)*

The main words for "time" in the New Testament are *chronos* and *kairos*. *Chronos* deals with the measure of time (quantity of time). *Kairos* has to do with timing being right (quality of time).

Why was Jesus so concerned with *kairos*, with timing being right? He didn't want to get out of sync with God the Father. If He stayed in the public eye too long, if He turned up the heat too fast, the hatred of the religious leaders would be brought to the boiling point too soon, and He would die on the cross ahead of schedule. Thinking of the cross, He said to His brothers: *"The world cannot hate you, but it hates me because I testify that what it does is evil." (John 7:7)*

The way of the world is doing what you want, when you want. In contrast, Jesus came to die on the cross at just the right time, in God's time. One key to being fully alive in Jesus is waiting for God's timing. Even when it's hard. Even when it kills you.

> *"I am not yet going up to this Feast, because for me the right time [kairos] has not yet come" (John 7:8b).*

Waiting for God's time is hard for me. God is so "not in a hurry," that a thousand years to us is a day to Him. In the New Living Translation of John 7:6-14, the words "right time" come up twice, the word "anytime," comes up once, and the words "not yet" come up once.

I don't like hearing the words "not yet" from heaven. Be that as it may, I know that waiting is a key to *kairos*—that sweetest of all spots where my time intersects with God's time, and the temporal kisses the eternal. If I submit my life and my schedule to God, He leads me to the *kairos. There is a time for everything, and a season for activity under the heavens. (Ecclesiastes 3:1)*

Submitting to God's timing is one key to being fully alive. *Kairos* is life-time!

Life Challenge: Think of one area in your life where God might be saying "not yet," and tell Him you are willing to wait for His *kairos.*

42
GOOD JUDGMENT

JUDGE HEART FIRST, head next.

JOHN 7:15-24

I was raised in a home with authentic, Christ-following parents. In high school, I decided I wanted to be popular more than I wanted to please God, so I turned my heart away from Him. Within a year or so, my head had turned away as well. I came to disbelieve the things I had been taught about God and chose a different lifestyle.

Years later, when I came back to faith heart first, it was hard for my head to follow. I believed some, but I needed major help with my unbelief. It took a lot of time in the Bible and in books by Christian apologists to change my mind.

Speaking of minds, the Jews in today's reading were amazed at the intellect of Jesus, considering that He lacked a seminary diploma. *Jesus answered, "My teaching is not my own. It comes from him who sent me. If anyone chooses to do God's will, he will find out whether my teaching comes from God or whether I speak on my own" (John 7:16-17).*

Some of those listening to Jesus said, "He's a fraud," and others said, "He's from God." Which is it? How does a person decide? Amazingly,

Jesus said that determining to do God's will comes *before* knowing His truth and experiencing His reality.

For six months I tried to come back to God 'head-first', while withholding part of my heart. God didn't begin to reveal His reality to me until I said sincerely, "I will do whatever You ask me to do—if You will show yourself to be real to me." And He did just that.

God showed Himself to me as a relational God, not a religious God. Jesus revealed the heart of the Father by healing a man on the Sabbath. When the religionists claimed His actions proved He was not from God, He said, *"Why are you angry with me for healing the whole man on the Sabbath?" (John 7:23).*

The God that Jesus revealed made rules (like Sabbath-keeping) because He loved people and wanted to help them thrive—be more alive. How could someone like Jesus, someone committed to helping people be more alive, not be from God? I love the way the Lord finished this dialog: *"Don't be nitpickers; use your head—and heart!—to discern what is right, to test what is authentically right" (John 7:24, MSG).*

Align your heart with God's heart and involve your heart in making judgments. Judging with all head and no heart will give you a big head and a small heart.

Life Action: Think of one time when you made a heart-first judgment about someone or something.

43
KNOW LIFE

DO YOU KNOW that you don't know?

John 7:25-36

I got lost once, late in the day, out in the wilderness in Eastern Oregon. The night before the temperature had dropped to ten above zero, and as the sun set, the mercury was once again headed for the deep-freeze. New to the area, I was totally disoriented. Thank God, a friend found me just in time.

I got lost because my GPS batteries had died—and with a weak sense of direction, I need all the help I can get. Unlike me, Jesus knew exactly where He came from (from God the Father) and where He was going (back to the Father).

The Jewish leaders thought Jesus came from the devil, that He was a spiritual Pied Piper leading the crowds down the wrong path. Some of those marching behind Him thought He might be the Messiah, but there was one thing that puzzled them. Tradition had it that the Messiah would just show up out of *nowhere*—and they knew that Jesus had come from Nazareth. It was 'know where' versus 'nowhere'. "The miracles Jesus keeps doing appear to be a real sign of special, divine life," they reasoned. *"But we know where this man is from; when the Christ comes, no one will know where he is from" (John 7:27).*

What they thought they knew barred the door to what they needed to know. Jesus replied, *"Yes, you know me, and you know where I am from. I am not here on my own, but he who sent me is true. You do not know him…" (John 7:28).*

Read between the lines. Jesus was saying, in effect, "It's sad you don't know *where* I'm from. It's tragic you don't know *Who* sent me here. If you really knew God the Father, you would recognize Me, His only begotten Son. You can't seem to comprehend that I was with the Father in heaven before I was born into humanity in Bethlehem. And you'll never know what you need to know until you admit what you don't know."

> *"And this is the way to have eternal life—to know you, the only true God, and Jesus Christ, the one you sent to earth" (John 17:3, NLT).*

The point is, if you think you have life all figured out, "knowing" may actually be a detriment to experiencing full aliveness. We all need divine directional assistance to locate real and lasting life. Ask God for help. Without help, you might freeze to death in a lonely place.

Life Question: Think of one thing you don't know but know that *He* knows. Tell Him.

44

BIG GULP

YOU DON'T HAVE TO be spiritually dehydrated.

John 7:37-39

On the last and greatest day of the Feast, Jesus stood and said in a loud voice, "If anyone is thirsty, let him come to me and drink" (John 7:37).

I was out with some friends hunting elusive birds called chukars on a very hot October day. We were five miles from our pickup and we'd forgotten to bring water. I found a marshy place where cows had trampled a little spring and was so desperately thirsty that I drank some brownish-yellow water that was in a cow's hoof-print. That afternoon as we headed home, I stopped in the tiny burg of Mitchell to buy and gulp a Big Gulp.

As soon as I got home, I called a doctor friend who got me some anti-giardia pills. I was surprised they worked, and I didn't get giardia. But looking back on that incident just amazes me. How could I have been so desperate, so foolish? Thirst can drive you to do things you didn't think you would ever do.

On the last day of the Feast of Tabernacles, the priests would lead a procession from the temple to the pool of Siloam, where they would take a pitcher, fill it with water from the pool, and pour it out ceremoniously to memorialize Moses striking the rock in the wilderness just before water gushed out for a desperately dehydrated nation (Numbers 20). As the priests piously poured out the water, Jesus stole the show by yelling out: *"If anyone is thirsty, let him come to me and drink" (John 7:37).*

Today as I read that verse, it dawned on me for the first time that the living water comes from the heart of Jesus. In John 16:7, Jesus promised that after He went away, He would send the Spirit. The river that comes from the heart of the Lord Jesus is *the Spirit of Life* (see John 7:39). Wow. Because Jesus sent the Spirit of Life, we don't have to be dehydrated! *"The Spirit alone gives eternal life" (John 6:63, NLT) "...Anyone who wants to; let him come and drink the Water of Life without charge" (Revelation 22:17, TLB).*

In his book, *Selling Water by the River* (Jericho Books), Shane Hipps highlights the word "IF" in verse 38: "This gift of eternal life is only a possibility for people, not a certainty. It comes with a condition. In John 7:37 Jesus begins his proclamation by saying '*If* anyone is thirsty, let him come to me and drink.' The first condition is to be thirsty. The experience of eternal life is exclusively reserved for thirsty people." Are you thirsty?

Life Action: Scriptures challenge us to *keep being filled* with the Holy Spirit (Ephesians 5:18). When was the last time you took a big gulp from the Living River? How about now?

45
LIFE OF SIN

GOD WOULD RATHER FORGIVE us than condemn us.

JOHN 7:53-8:11

Jesus went to the Mount of Olives, one of His favorite places to pray and recharge. At dawn, He walked to the temple court, where He sat to teach His growing audience. In mid-sentence, the Pharisees brought a woman who had been caught in the act of adultery and stood her in front of Him, greatly pleased to present Him with an impossible situation. *"Teacher, this woman was caught in the act of adultery. In the Law Moses commanded us to stone such women. Now what do you say?" (John 8:4-5).* If he said, "Stone her," he would lose His followers who loved Him for His compassion and forgiveness. If He had said, "Don't stone her," He would be accused of rejecting Mosaic law and lose credibility with the orthodox.

When I read this my first question was, "Where's the guy? Doesn't it take two to tango?" The accusers really didn't care anything about justice; they just wanted to trap Jesus and put Him to death. And on that day, they thought they finally had him. Instead of stepping into their trap, however, Jesus stooped to write something on the ground. Scholars have long debated what Jesus wrote that day, and we really have no way of knowing. We do know, however, that His words convicted the accusers and the crowd. The words formed by His finger somehow pointed a finger at each and every one of them.

> *When they kept on questioning him, he straightened up and said to them, "If any one of you is without sin, let him be the first to throw a stone at her" (John 8:7).*

Jesus stooped again and wrote on the ground. I'd love to know what it was. If I had been there, I'll bet my curiosity would have been followed closely by my conviction. One by one, oldest to youngest, the people began to put down their stones and walk away in silence, until only Jesus and the woman were left. *Jesus straightened up and asked her, "Woman, where are they? Has no one condemned you?" "No one, sir," she said. "Then neither do I condemn you," Jesus declared. "Go now and leave your life of sin" (John 8:10-11).*

This story brings back to me the words Jesus spoke to Nicodemus late one night: *"For God did not send his Son into the world to condemn the world, but to save the world through him …Light has come into the world, but men loved darkness instead of light…" (John 3:17, 19).* Jesus is the light of the world, but I see Him as more like a lamp in a lighthouse than like a policeman's spotlight that catches a wrong-doer in the act. His light doesn't judge, it reveals and invites us into His life.

Life Question: Can you think of one secret thing Jesus could write about your life that would cause you to let go of criticism and be more compassionate?

46
LIGHT OF LIFE

JESUS is the light of life.

JOHN 8:12

It was dark and the battery on our pickup was stone dead.

Now what?

Stranded in a remote, very sparsely populated region near the base of the Steens Mountains in southeastern Oregon, we had no choice but to go looking for help. We began walking toward the light from a distant ranch house. We guessed that the house was ten miles north across the vast sagebrush flatland, but after walking for an hour, the light still looked ten miles away.

Then we saw a glint of light on the hillside to the west. It was moonlight reflecting off the window of a pickup canopy. After a fifteen-minute climb up the hillside, we called out to the bird hunter sleeping inside. He sat up and turned on the overhead light in his canopy. An hour later his battery revived ours and we headed home.

I've thought about that shimmer of reflected moonlight many times since. That bit of reflected light represented hope and help to three extremely tired men on that dark night.

When Jesus spoke again to the people, he said, "I am the light of the world. Whoever follows me will never walk in darkness but will have the light of life" (John 8:12).

Jesus said, in effect, 'I am the light of this spiritually dark world.' He reflects God's aliveness just as a full moon reflects the light of the sun. And His reflected aliveness provides direction for seekers who would otherwise be lost in the darkness.

When I was a teenager, I remember standing on Sixth Avenue in Portland, Oregon when I suddenly looked up and saw a sign that said: "I am the light of the world." I remember thinking, *I wish I could believe that.* But at that moment I didn't, and life seemed dark and hopeless.

Six months later, I saw an appealing brightness—a glint of reflected light—in the eyes of Steve, a high school friend who was bold enough to talk plainly with me about the One who claimed to be *the light that leads to life (John 8:12, NLT).* I started by reading the gospel of John, and the words of Jesus came alive, indeed seemed almost neon to me. I've since learned to prize the reflections of God's aliveness in His Word and in this world.

Life Challenge: Do you currently see a reflection of God's aliveness in someone's life? Are you willing to tell that person what you see?

47

CAN YOU SEE ME NOW?

GOD is light.

John 8:13-20

When Jesus said that He was *"living light" (John 8:12, TLB)*, the Pharisees retorted, "We don't see it that way. In fact, we don't believe You."

"You're blind to the light of life in Me," Jesus was telling them, "because you judge by human standards. You just look at the surface of people and miss the substance."

He went on to say, *"I don't make judgments like that. But even if I did, my judgment would be true because I wouldn't make it out of the narrowness of my experience but in the largeness of the One who sent me, the Father"* (John 8:16b, MSG).

A few days ago, I was trying to read the small print on a medicine bottle and could only make out about half the words. Then I went over and stood directly under the light. It helped a lot. My judgment is better—I see things better—when the light is brighter.

The Bible says, "God is light." Jesus, being so close to God the Father, looked at people and situations in the light of God's illumination. The Pharisees misread Jesus and misread God the Father because they saw things in the shadowed light of their own selfishness and smallness, coming from a 'I follow the rules, so I'm OK' mindset. Indeed, these hyper-religious specialists were God-blind.

> *They said, "Where is this so-called Father of yours?" Jesus said, "You're looking right at me and you don't see me. How do you expect to see the Father? If you knew me, you would at the same time know the Father" (John 8:19, MSG).*

These scriptures are teaching me that the closer I get to God, the better I see God in Jesus, the better I see myself, and the better I see others. God's judgment is good judgment. He knows so much more than I know. He sees so much more than I see.

Remembering this makes me more inclined to ask God, "What do You see here—in this situation, in this set of circumstances—that You want me to see?" I need to get closer to the light before I try to read the label.

Life Challenge: Is there something you are trying to decide or discern these days? Remember that as you get closer to God, your perception improves.

48
LIFE FROM ABOVE

WHEN I DON'T UNDERSTAND what God is saying about life, He patiently puts it another way.

JOHN 8:21-30

God dressed in skin was standing right in front of them. They didn't recognize Him, so Jesus...*went over the same ground again. "I'm leaving and you are going to look for me, but you're missing God in this and are headed for a dead end" (John 8:21a, MSG).*

When Jesus talked about going somewhere that they couldn't go, they thought He might be speaking of suicide. But He was talking about going to God the Father, going back to ultimate aliveness. "You can't reach God and ultimate aliveness," Jesus said, 'because you've misjudged Me. I'm not just going to ultimate aliveness, *I am* the one and only way to get there.'

Jesus was speaking to people who were physically alive but spiritually dead. Physical life is terminal. Spiritual life, life offered by God through Jesus, is a longer, deeper, higher form of life. Spiritual life is life from above. If Jesus hadn't come from above to bring us life from above, we couldn't be born from above and end up living above, happily ever after.

He continued, "You are from below; I am from above…
if you do not believe that I am the one I claim to be, you
will indeed die in your sins" (John 8:23a, 24a).

When Jesus spoke of "dying in sin," He wasn't just talking about *why* they would die (they sinned) but *how* they would die. Sin is anything that disconnects us (partially or completely) from God. Jesus is the way to stay connected to God. If I don't believe in Jesus, I miss the only way to be connected to God's eternal aliveness. Jesus said it plainly: "If you don't believe and receive Me, you're on a dead-end road." But *They still didn't get it… So Jesus tried again (8:27a, MSG).*

I love God's persistence. I love how He explains it yet another way when I don't get it the first, second, or third time. I love how He kept after me, even after I had turned my back on Him. *When he put it in these terms, many people decided to believe (John 8:30, MSG).*

Me, too.

Life Challenge: Do you know someone who seems blind to something that is obvious to you? Instead of giving up on that person, ask God to help you "put it another way."

49
TRUTH DECAY

TRUTH…or consequences.

JOHN 8:31-47

Some of the people listening to Jesus' teachings were beginning to conclude that He was the real deal. *To the Jews who had believed him, Jesus said, "If you hold to my teaching, you are really my disciples. Then you will know the truth, and the truth will set you free" (John 8:31-32).*

Believing is a process. The NIV says here '**had believed**.' The Living Bible says they '**began believing.**' The Message says, they '**claimed to believe.**' Faith can be faked, and believers can become unbelievers.

It's common to hear the truth, grab hold, but then let it slip away. True belief is holding on for dear life. Only then does God's truth set free you from the lies within you and around you. Why then, do we let go of the truth?

Two years ago, our family was boating at Shasta Lake in northern California. As we pulled up to the dock, I put one leg over onto the boards. Just then the boat pulled away from the dock. I did the splits, injuring my right hip. Why had I held on to both the boat and the dock? Because I had my cell phone in my pocket and didn't want it to get wet!

When push came to shove, I couldn't decide which way to jump. And my indecision was painful!

That's what it's like when we try to hold onto both the truth of Christ and our own priorities and agenda at the same time. At some point, we'll have to jump one way or the other. Yes, holding onto the Lord's way may bring some pain before it brings freedom. As someone once said, "The truth will set you free, but it might make you miserable first." Maybe that is why so many of Christ's critics, somewhere in their lives, let go of the truth.

The critics told Jesus that they were descendants of Abraham and in spite of Rome's oppression, totally free spirits. Then Jesus told them the truth about their lies. They were actually caught in a death trap. He went on to tell them that if they had been really connected with the living God, they would have recognized His totally truthful Son. (Jesus says "I tell you the truth" thirty times in the book of John.)

'The truth is,' Jesus reproved the religious leaders, 'as children of the devil and slaves of death, you will eventually kill Me, even though I told you the truth that I heard from God.' At that, they accused Him of being a lying lunatic. When you call the One who totally personifies truth a liar, you've got a terrible case of truth decay!

Life Question: What is the worst case of truth decay you've ever seen in our culture? In your family? In yourself?

50

I AM

JESUS: Is He who He claims to be?

JOHN 8:48-59

Reading the book of John is like sitting on a jury that is deciding whether Jesus is who He claims to be. Within the pages of the gospel, Jesus repeats the words *I am* over and over again. *I am the way...I am the truth...I am the light...I am the good shepherd...I am the door.* And on it goes.

The word translated "I am" in the New Testament is the Greek word *ego*. In English, ego means self. The Lord's ego statements led some of those who encountered Him to the conclusion that He was a self-obsessed mental case—or an ego-maniac: *The Jews then said, "That clinches it. We were right all along when we called you a Samaritan and said you were crazy—demon-possessed!" (John 8:48, MSG).*

"You're acting like you're the judge," Jesus said, but *"God is going to glorify me. He is the true judge" (John 8:50b, NLT).* 'God is going to rule in my favor. Indeed, He already has. And since God is Life, those who hold on to what I say about myself, about life, will *never have to look death in the face' (John 8:51, MSG).*

They asked Jesus, *"Who do you think you are?" (John 8:53).* "I am I

AM," He told them. His message was 'I am unstoppable, uninterrupted Aliveness. I am eternal.'

'You're nuts,' they said. 'Abraham, our father in the faith, is the greatest man we know of, and he died.'

> *"Believe me," said Jesus, "I am who I am long before Abraham was anything" (John 8:58, MSG).*

Get that? Jesus claimed that He was in existence before Abraham was born. He claimed to be *the* "I Am," a Jewish title kept exclusively for God. "I Am" is eternal aliveness. Jesus is God, and God is ultimate, unstoppable aliveness—*all three* tenses of existence at once and forever.

The whole court case hinges on the issue of aliveness. Jesus claims to BE aliveness, to HAVE aliveness, and to GIVE aliveness. If He had just cooled that aliveness thing, maybe He wouldn't have had to experience death by crucifixion. But even that was, for Him, only temporary. As Jesus summed it up for John in the book of Revelation, *"I am He who lives, and was dead, and behold, I am alive forevermore" (Revelation 1:18, NKJV).*

Life Challenge: Claiming to be the source of eternal aliveness, Jesus said, *"Believe me" (John 8:58, MSG).* Do you? If you do, tell Him now, and tell someone else today that you believe Jesus.

51
VIEWPOINT

BE LIKE JESUS today. Look for someone to bless.

John 9:1-4

Richard is in our Thursday morning men's Bible study group. Born prematurely, he and his twin brother were placed in an incubator and given too much oxygen. That critical mistake robbed them both of eyesight for life.

That's a human tragedy, of course, but the truth is that you and I lack sight too. All of us lack the ability to see all that may happen (foresight), is happening (insight) and has happened (hindsight). Since Adam and Eve, we've all been born partially blind. There is so much we don't see!

One day Jesus and His disciples encountered a man who couldn't see. He was... *a man blind from birth. His disciples asked him, "Rabbi, who sinned, this man or his parents, that he was born blind?" (John 9:1-2).* The disciples believed that sickness of any kind was the result of sin, and they were looking for someone to blame.

"Neither this man nor his parents sinned," said Jesus, "but this happened so that the works of God might be displayed in him" (John 9:3). Jesus introduced an entirely new concept here: Sometimes God uses difficult things in our lives to display His glory, His irrepressible aliveness! I wonder

how often we do what they did and look at things from the wrong angle. We look for someone to blame when we should be looking for someone to bless.

Jesus said the man's blindness was an opportunity for the "works of God" to be on display in his life. What are the works of God? The works of God make people more alive in Christ, and God wants to put such works on display in our lives.

> "As long as it is day, we must do the works of him who sent me. Night is coming, when no one can work" (John 9:4).

In today's passage, Jesus sticks with the subject of sight, day and night, dark and light. Spiritual night is living without light. Living without Jesus in my life is living without light. The ultimate night is hell. Since God is not in hell, hell is pitch black. Where God is, however, even pitch black becomes bright light!

Life Challenge: Look for at least one person you could blame today, and bless them instead, in Jesus' Name. Thank Him for helping you *see* the opportunity to be a blessing.

52
LIGHT OF THE WORLD

THERE'S MORE TO SEE when you look at Jesus.

JOHN 9:5

I guess "dumb blonde" jokes are politically incorrect these days, but there is one harmless little story about a golden-hair that still makes me chuckle. Blondie said she wanted to go on a spaceship and land on the sun. "That's crazy," her husband protested. "You'd be fried to a crisp." "No way," his wife responded, "I'd go at night!"

Light is mentioned 21 times in John's gospel. John called Jesus *the light of men* (1:4), *the Life-Light* (1:5, MSG), *the True light* (1:9), *the clear light* (9:39, MSG), and on it goes.

In John 9:5, Jesus declared, **"While I am in the world, I am the light of the world."**

Notice the definite article. Not *a* light but *the* light. What an audacious claim! As we all know, light represents hope, direction, illumination, attraction, and life itself. Jesus is claiming to be all of those things for anyone who sees Him for who He is. He is the whole spectrum of deep, unending life.

If you're discussing light with a scientific person, he or she may speak in terms of electromagnetic radiation—radiant energy with wavelengths ranging from one billionth of a meter to over 60,000 miles. What's more, our eyes only perceive a tiny sliver of that light. That minuscule shard of light visible to us is light with a wavelength ranging from four hundred billionths of a meter (Ultraviolet light) seven hundred billionths of a meter (infrared light). Think of it like this: If a cable stretched all the way around the earth represented total light (every wavelength of electromagnetic radiation), visible light would be but a scratch of a pencil or pen on that cable. When it comes to light, there's so much more than what we see!

When the apostle John saw the Lord's glory shine through His earth-suit veil on the Mount of Transfiguration, he fell face down in shock and awe. If you and I saw His entire wavelength, His radiant glory, our eyeballs would pop like popcorn.

Jesus is the light of the world. He is hope, illumination, direction, attraction—and so very much beyond what we could ever express! Jesus is life. He's the life-light, God's invisible aliveness made visible. Put on your sunglasses and take a closer look.

Life Challenge: Ask Jesus Christ to open the eyes of your heart and show you something about Himself this week that you've never noticed before.

53
EYE-OPENER

EYE-OPENERS change life.

JOHN 9:6-15

My mom was almost blind when she passed away. An eye doctor diagnosed early glaucoma and macular degeneration in my own eyes fifteen years ago. The doctor's good care has helped me hold steady visually since diagnosis, but I will tell you this: Eyesight is incredibly precious.

In today's Scripture we read: *Having said this, he spit on the ground, made some mud with the saliva, and put it on the man's eyes (John 9:6).* Having said this—that He was the light of the world—Jesus prepares to act in line with His claim and give the blind man new, exciting exposure to light.

"Go," he told him, "wash in the Pool of Siloam." …So the man went and washed, and came home seeing (John 9:7). Jesus pointed the man toward a richer, fuller, brighter life. Why didn't Jesus just say "See"? Could it be—for the blind man and for us—that humility and doing something by faith usually precedes healing?

His neighbors and those who had formerly seen him begging asked, "Isn't this the same man who used to sit and beg?" (John 9:8). The healed man himself confirmed that he used to be blind but was no longer. When

Jesus is making you more alive, you walk away from so many "used to be's." You're more than a 'human being'; you're a 'human being' becoming a new kind of human. Jesus helps people see what they never saw before and be who they've never been before. *"How then were your eyes opened?" they demanded. He replied, "The man they call Jesus..."* (John 9:10-11a).

Going to college was an eye-opener for me. As was traveling to Uganda. So was encountering Jesus in my senior year of high school. Can you think of an experience that was an eye-opener for you? Are you praying for a friend or family member who needs an eye-opener?

The apostle Paul tells us that *Satan, who is the god of this world, has blinded the minds of those who don't believe. They are unable to see the glorious light of the Good News (2 Corinthians 4:4a, NLT).* A blind mind is even more life-depleting than dysfunctional eyes.

Life Question: Can you think of one negative characteristic of your life that "used to be" but is no longer, since you saw who Jesus is?

54

GOD REVEALING

IF YOU REALLY SEE GOD, you'll see Him helping and healing people.

John 9:16-23

Have you ever seen a no-see-um? No-see-ums are a nasty tribe of biting midges that are so tiny as to be almost invisible. When I read what the New Testament says about the religious leaders of Jesus' day, the Pharisees and Sadducees, I think of them as *Phari-no-see-ums* and *Sad-you-no-see-ums*. The One sent from God was right in front of them, but they could not-see-Him.

Some of the Pharisees said, "Obviously, this man [Jesus] can't be from God. He doesn't keep the Sabbath" (John 9:16a, MSG). Jesus wouldn't stay in their six-day-box because God never takes a day off from helping people. *Others countered, "How can a bad man do miraculous, God-revealing things like this?" There was a split in their ranks (John 9:16b, MSG).*

A split in their ranks? I would call it a split between those with vision and those with no vision. What was a dark eclipse for some was like breaking daylight for others.

Some were beginning to see Jesus as doing God-revealing things. In other words, they saw Him doing things that revealed a life-giving, people-helping God. They saw God-in-Jesus working overtime to make people physically, psychologically, socially, spiritually, presently and eternally more alive.

Ready to pounce on any misstatement, the religious leaders asked the post-blind man who he thought Jesus was. The man replied simply, *"He is a prophet" (John 9:17b)*. Some people may see Jesus as a prophet, a Higher Power, or an inspired teacher before they see Him as God's Son.

The newly healed blind man may not have been sure who Jesus was at that point, but he was certainly aware of God's goodness—and knew that what Jesus had done for him had vastly increased his quality of life. For the moment, that was okay. It's alright to be partly right about Jesus—if you're open to finding out more.

Flustered, the religionists tried to pull the puppet strings of the seeing man's parents and succeeded. Instead of defending their son or his healer, the parents threw their boy under the bus and cowardly replied, "Ask him." It makes me want to check my own back for a yellow streak. Fear of man can blind us to God-revealing things happening right in front of our faces.

Life Challenge: Ask God to help you do at least one life-giving, people-helping, God-revealing thing today.

55

BLIND DATE

UNTIL I SEE JESUS...for who He is, every day on my calendar is a blind date.

JOHN 9:24-34

A second time they summoned the man who had been blind (John 9:24a). The former blind man had a court date, but thank God, it wasn't a blind date. They made him swear on the Old Testament to tell the truth, the whole truth, and nothing but—what they wanted him to say! Obviously, they had made up their minds already, and a closed mind is a blind mind. *"Give glory to God," they said. "We know this man [Jesus] is a sinner" (John 9:24b).* The man with restored sight truly did give glory to God. Men and women who are fully alive in Christ just naturally bring Him glory.

He replied, "Whether he is a sinner or not, I don't know. One thing I do know. I was blind but now I see!" (John 9:25). Don't you love that answer? 'Hey guys, just think about this. I CAN SEE! I've been blind from birth, living in a world of total darkness. But now I see the world in living color. Can't you see that? Maybe you're the ones who are blind!'

I don't know where this man got his backbone, but it wasn't from his parents. And when the leaders tried to pull his religious puppet strings as they had done to his mom and dad, they found that the puppet strings had been cut and wouldn't work. Jesus Himself had set the man free, and that made these prideful bullies were very, very angry.

"You illegitimate bastard, you!" they shouted. *"Are you trying to teach us?"* And they threw him out *(John 9:34, TLB)*. The once-blind man, largely untaught, was teachable. The religionists, highly taught, were pretty much unteachable. One huge key to becoming more alive is being a teachable, life-long learner. Too often, I'm afraid, I'm not as teachable as I should be, but I don't see it until I look back. My hindsight is better than my insight.

How teachable are you today?

Life Challenge: Rank your current teachability level between 0, *unteachable,* and 10, *totally teachable.* Add two to your score and use that for your goal today.

56

EYE WITNESS

ADMIT YOUR NEED for more exposure to truth.

John 9:35-41

I learned about cameras in the third grade. I built a crude camera by putting a pinhole in a small cardboard box and capturing an inverted picture on photographic film. Even in those early days, I remember being intrigued by the concept of light and exposure. In John chapter 9, the former blind man was first exposed to the light in Jesus—and then exposed to the darkness of spiritual pride in the religious leaders of his day.

Jesus heard that they had thrown him out and went and found him. He asked him, "Do you believe in the Son of Man?" The man said, "Point him out to me, sir, so that I can believe in him" (John 9:35-36, MSG) The newly created visionary looked for something beyond blind faith. He asked for more insight, more evidence, more revelation, more truth.

When I walked away from God as a young man, my life became empty and dark. I wanted to believe in God again, but no longer felt it was logical or feasible. Finally, I asked God for a specific sign of His reality, and at that very point Jesus began to reintroduce Himself to me.

I have a friend, Stephen, who has an effective ministry in Christian apologetics. Stephen was a staunch agnostic until he took up a friend on her challenge to spend a year researching reasons for faith or lack of faith. As time went on, Stephen discovered many reasons to believe—in nature, in scripture, and all around him. He'd just needed to stop and look. He'd needed someone to point out a few of those reasons to him.

Jesus said, "You're looking right at him. Don't you recognize my voice?" (John 9:37, MSG). This man was blind when Jesus sent him off to the pool where he received glorious eyesight. He had heard Jesus' voice, but up until that point, he hadn't actually seen Jesus. He had been trying to believe in a person he had never seen. When Jesus pointed to Himself, the man became an eyewitness to eternal aliveness in a human body. (9:38)

This is a beautiful picture of what some people call "progressive revelation." If we acknowledge our blindness and crave better insight, God will give us more revelation. On the other hand, if we pretend to have 20/20 knowledge already, what small amount of sight we have will further decrease. *"Those who have made a great pretense of seeing will be exposed as blind" (John 9:39b, MSG).*

Life Question: In what area would you say, "I am partially blind…but I'd like to see more"?

57
SAFE

IF I HAVE JESUS...I have all that I need.

John 10:1-11

Jesus had just exposed a crowd of religious know-it-alls. They had imagined themselves to be wise and clear-sighted, but Jesus called them blind. And then on top of that, He called them thieves, too! *"Very truly I tell you...anyone who does not enter the sheep pen by the gate, but climbs in by some other way, is a thief and a robber" (John 10:1).*

In stark contrast to the sheep-thieves, Jesus claimed to be the good shepherd (vs 11) and the sheep-gate. (vs 7) In my office at home, I have a photograph of a large rock-wall sheep corral, built many decades ago by shepherds in the wilderness near Owyhee Reservoir in eastern Oregon. The rock wall is about 150 yards in circumference and four feet high. Its gate is just a six-foot wide opening in the rock wall. Shepherds would put the sheep in the corral and lie down in the opening. To any wolves or sheep-nappers hoping to sneak and grab a lamb, the shepherd was saying, "Over my dead body."

The Good Shepherd lays down His life for the sheep, and His sheep (including the healed man spoken of in chapter 9) *"... follow him because they know his voice" (John 10:4b).* Mid-eastern shepherds would lead their flocks from the front, calling out to individual sheep by name. I like that. The government knows me by my Social Security number, but the Good Shepherd knows the name that He gave me.

It is one thing for a sheep to hear the shepherd's voice, and another for the sheep to understand His direction. *Jesus told this simple story, but they had no idea what he was talking about. So he tried again. "I'll be explicit then. I am the gate for the sheep. Anyone who goes through me will be cared for — will freely go in and out, and will find pasture" (John 10:7-9 MSG).*

I love how the text says that Jesus "tried again." He has tried again (and again and again) with me a thousand times over. He is persistently merciful, and He keeps me safe and sound and well-nourished. My thinking jumps from here to Psalm 23, which speaks of still waters and green pastures. The Shepherd offers His sheep provision, protection, direction, correction, and restoration. He is everything I need. I shall not be in want.

Baaa… baaa…blessing.

Life Question: What do you think Jesus meant by "come in and go out and find pasture"? (Does it relate to the next verse, John 10:10?)

58
DEATH AND LIFE

JESUS CAME TO HELP you and me experience deep, unending life.

JOHN 10:10

The gospel of John is full of signs of life. You might call John 10:10, near the middle of John's testimony, the spinal cord of the book: *"The thief comes only to steal and kill and destroy; I have come that they may have life, and have it to the full" (John 10:10).*

We really have no concept of how much Satan, the thief, hates aliveness. He has come to steal away and stamp out life wherever he sees it. *Then Jesus said to them, "I ask you, which is lawful on the Sabbath: to do good or to do evil, to save life or to destroy it?" (Luke 6:9).* See that? Doing good is saving life. Doing evil is destroying life.

What is true in the New Testament of the Bible is also true in the Old Testament. In the book of Genesis, we read: *"Don't you see, you planned evil against me but God used those same plans for my good, as you see all around you right now—life for many people" (Genesis 50:20, MSG).*

Jesus came to do good, to give us deep, unending aliveness. **"I have come that they may have life...."** There are many dimensions of good and evil. Good is light, evil is darkness. Good is truth, evil is deception. Good is pure, evil is corrupt. Good is life, evil is death. The second half of John 10:10 speaks of good, while the first half speaks of evil. All through the Bible, *good* is anything that helps people connect with God's aliveness. In contrast, *evil* is anything that disconnects people from God's aliveness.

Addressing the subject of life itself, Jesus spoke of those who wanted to have more life, **"... have it to the full."** What is this full life that Jesus spoke of? The New Living Testament calls it "a rich and satisfying life." The Living Bible calls it "life in all its fullness." The King James translation calls it "abundant life." The Message paraphrase calls it "more and better life than they ever dreamed of." Plentiful, rich, vital, lavish life.

Interested?

Life Question: Set your mind to do one good thing today—one thing that helps someone become a bit more alive.

59

SACRIFICED LIFE

JESUS LIVED a "you-first" life.

JOHN 10:11-21

Jesus said, *"I am the good shepherd. The good shepherd lays down his life for the sheep" (John 10:11).*

What does "lays down his life" mean? The Message paraphrase says, "…puts the sheep before himself, sacrifices himself if necessary." In other words, He lets go of His aliveness in order to make more aliveness available to His sheep - to us. This stands in contrast to the thief (Satan) and to most of the religious leaders (hired hands) of Christ's day. *"The hired hand … sees the wolf coming, he abandons the sheep and runs away. Then the wolf attacks the flock and scatters it. The man runs away because he… cares nothing for the sheep" (John 10:12-13).*

You would think being a sheep would be a fairly simple job description, but there are complications, aren't there? Besides being mentally deficient, sheep face challenges from thieves, cowardly hired hands, and hungry wolves. When Jesus was arrested, the gospel of Mark says that the sheep (His followers) quickly scattered (Mark 14:27). Sheep become confused and vulnerable when they scatter. Have you ever been part of a "scattered" flock? A scattered fellowship? A scattered family?

The Good Shepherd said, *"I lay down my life for the sheep"* (John *10:15b*). That's quite a contrast to the hired hand who **"cares nothing for the sheep."** Through the years of our lives, you and I will encounter both kinds of leaders—from selfless to selfish. Selfish leaders, from pimps to politicians, use people. Good leaders love people and lay down their lives for people.

"The reason my Father loves me is that I lay down my life...of my own accord" (John *10:17a-18a*). What does Jesus mean here? What does God love about Jesus being willing to die—to be disconnected from God's rich aliveness—in our place? God the Father is a *lay-down-My-Son-God*. He is a *lay-down-My-life-God*. When He sees His only begotten Son living His likeness on this planet, He loves it.

> *This kind of talk caused another split in the Jewish ranks*
> *(John 10:19a MSG).*

Of course, it did! Jesus' words always have and always will "split" people. Sheep from goats. Believers from scoffers. Wheat from tares. Light from dark. Life from death. One group of those who heard Him that day said He was *"demon-possessed and raving mad"* (John *10:19*). Another group said the opposite, that no demon-possessed man could speak with such wisdom and open the eyes of a blind man.

When it came to Jesus, there was no middle ground that day.

There never is.

Life Question: Can you name one good shepherd you've known, other than Jesus? Tell someone about that lay-down-your-life person today.

60
SHEEP

HIS SHEEP never perish.

JOHN 10:22-30

When Jesus was in Jerusalem for the Feast of Dedication (Hanukkah), *The Jews gathered around him, saying, "How long will you keep us in suspense? If you are the Christ, tell us plainly" (John 10:24).* The phrase translated "gathered around Him" means "encircled like wolves."

Jesus answered, "I did tell you, but you do not believe" (John 10:25a). I have a friend named Billy who is new to following Christ. Billy recently purchased a car for his estranged "ex." A few days ago he told me, "She hasn't shown interest in Jesus yet, but she is watching me. She can see the new goodness and aliveness in me."

Actions often out-speak words, don't they? Jesus said something similar: *"The miracles I do in my Father's name speak for me" (John 10:25b).* The miracles Jesus implemented contained messages about aliveness. Every miracle cried out "God cares about every aspect of your aliveness—social, emotional, mental, physical, spiritual."

He went on to say *"...but you do not believe because you are not my sheep. My sheep listen to my voice; I know them, and they follow me" (John 10:26-27).* One of the *I Am's* of Jesus in the book of John is ***"I Am The***

Life." Jesus' sheep listen to the voice of Life and follow in the footsteps of Life. I wonder how many times in an average day I hear His voice? How about you?

"I give them eternal life, and they shall never perish; no one can snatch them out of my hand" (John 10:28). Jesus again brings the conversation back to the subject of life. 'My sheep are protected from the life-destroyer. I speak life and give life, and those who follow Me are becoming more alive day by day.' The Lord's enemies understood all too well that only God can trump death and give eternal life. By making such statements, Jesus was claiming to be God. And then He removed all doubt by saying: *"I and the Father are one." (John 10:30).*

In other words, unquenchable, unstoppable aliveness is available from the Father through the Son.

Life Challenge: Think of one way you are (mentally, emotionally, socially, spiritually) more alive than you were a month ago. Thank the Good Shepherd.

61
GIVING ETERNAL LIFE

BELIEVE INTO His aliveness.

JOHN 10:31-42

By saying that anyone spiritually connected to Him was connected to eternal aliveness, Jesus claimed to be one with the Father. In response, the angry religionists filled their clips and got ready to gun Him down.

Jesus asked them which of His life-giving miracles had earned Him a death sentence. They replied that it wasn't the miracles that got Him in trouble, but rather His claim to be one with the Father. Jesus responded by saying that both His teachings and His miracles weren't actually His, but His Father's. *"Do not believe me unless I do what my Father does…"* *(John 10:37).* In other words, "You need to talk to God if you've got an issue with Me. I'm giving a new level of life—better, longer life—to those who believe I can. I'm doing exactly what the Father is doing. Can't you see the divinity? I'm helping, healing, forgiving, encouraging and caring. I'm giving life. Doesn't that remind you of Someone?"

What's that old expression? If it looks like a duck, quacks like a duck, and walks like a duck…it must be a duck!

"Then perhaps things will come together for you, and you'll see that not only are we doing the same thing, we are the same—Father and Son. He is in me; I am in him" (John 10:38, MSG).

My son Jeremy was, in a sense, in my loins before he was born. And some of my DNA and features are in him (poor boy).

Jesus' talk of oneness and being "in each other" screamed "blasphemy!" to the religious rule-keepers. They tried to seize Jesus, but it wasn't His time to punch out yet. He slipped away from the scene of strife and went to a rural area on the Jordan River. Those curious about life and hungry for the kind of life He spoke of followed Him there and listened to His words of life. *And in that place many believed in Jesus (John 10:42).*

Fourteen different verses in John contain the words *believe* and *life*. We believe our way into God-life. It only takes a tiny seed of true faith to believe into life (John 3:16).

Life Question: What do you think about the people who followed Jesus to the Jordan River and believed in Him in that place? Did they believe enough to possess eternal life? Do you?

62
GROUNDS FOR BELIEVING

EVERYONE has some grounds for belief.

JOHN 11:1-16

Lazarus, one of Jesus' closest friends, was deathly ill. Lazarus' two sisters, Martha and Mary, sent an urgent "come quick" message to Jesus. *When he heard this, Jesus said, "This sickness will not end in death" (John 11:4a).* What would look like an end would be transformed into a new beginning.

Yet when he heard that Lazarus was sick, he stayed where he was two more days (John 11:6). In place of "Yet," other translations say "In spite of that," "Surprisingly," and "But oddly." How often does God's timing seem odd to you? Do you think God actually enjoys surprising people, or is He just being God while we are not being God?

Two days later, Jesus and His men made the trip to Mary and Martha's home on the outskirts of Jerusalem. Before leaving, however, the disciples had questioned the wisdom of going back to where Jesus had so recently experienced a close brush with death.

Jesus answered, "Are there not twelve hours of daylight? A man who walks by day will not stumble, for he sees by this world's light. It is when he walks by night that he stumbles, for he has no light" (John 11:9-10). Jesus here equates "daylight" with sticking close to Him and perceiving what God is doing. He equates "stumbling" with drifting from Him and becoming confused about God's acts.

Then Jesus told the guys that Lazarus had fallen asleep and that He was going to wake His friend up. "Great," the disciples said, "if he's sleeping, he's getting better."

"Actually," the Lord finally told them, "he is DEAD." Dead. Dead. Dead. Not only "mostly dead" like the guy in the old movie *Princess Bride,* but totally dead.

And then He went on to say, *"Lazarus is dead, and for your sake I am glad I was not there, so that you may believe. But let us go to him." (John 11:14).* God loves to give us 'new grounds for believing.' In fact, that's what the book of John is all about (check out John 20:31).

Do some people have more grounds for believing than others? Yes, but everyone has *some* grounds. Whatever ground for faith God has given you, build something on it! Be honest about your doubts and exercise your faith. Keep believing even when it seems impossible. Don't put a period where God puts a comma.

Life Challenge: Can you think of one time you've been in the dark and stumbled recently? Get closer to Jesus. You'll see better.

63
KILLING DEATH

BELIEVE in order to live.

John 11:17-27

A friend of a friend was hunting birds on the rugged rim-rocks of eastern Oregon when he came up over a rise and saw his hunting dog hanging limp from the mouth of a cougar. He raised his gun, but it was too late. His prized dog was dead. The cat dropped its prey and ran off. Carrying his dog back to his truck was a tearful trek.

Like that mountain lion, death goes for life's jugular. When death clamped its jaws on Lazarus, a dear friend of Jesus, Jesus wasn't there on the scene to fight back. He did finally arrive, but he was four days late.

Jesus reminded Martha that her brother's death wasn't the end of his existence. *"Your brother will be raised up." Martha answered, "I know that he will be raised up in the resurrection at the end of time" (John 11:23-24, MSG).* In response, Jesus said, *"You don't have to wait for the End. I am, right now, Resurrection and Life" (John 11:25a, MSG).*

We tend to think of life as a biological or spiritual condition, but Jesus boldly claimed that life is a person. *He* is life. The Bible says that all things were created through Him. In other words, He is the source of all life, now and forever.

"I am, right now, Resurrection and Life." The "I ams" of Christ are woven through the gospel of John—and this might be the most mind-bending, death-defying "I am" of all. Talk about going for the kill! Here in Bethany, He grabbed death by the neck and bit down. *God went for the jugular when he sent his own Son (Romans 8:3a, MSG).*

Jesus went on to tell Martha, *"The one who believes in me, even though he or she dies, will live. And everyone who lives believing in me does not ultimately die at all" (John 11:25b-26a, MSG).* Note the next four words of Jesus; they are incredibly crucial. *"Do you believe this?" (John 11:26b, MSG).* Your eternal address will be determined by your answer.

Life Question: Everyone wants more and better life. Have you ever thought of 'better life' as being a person and not just a condition or a possession?

64

LORD, IF ONLY...

GOD IS BIGGER than your "if only's".

JOHN 11:28-38

Last week I pulled out of the hardware store parking lot onto a busy main road, heard tires squeal, and yelled *"NO!"* just before the front right bumper of my truck slapped a passing car. If only I had slowed down. If only I had paid closer attention.

"If only" makes a good whip. *If only I...If only you...If only someone...If only God....* Snap, snap, snap goes the whip. Have you ever been at a funeral and had those words "If only..." float into your mind?

When Mary reached the place where Jesus was and saw him, she fell at his feet and said, "Lord, if you had been here, my brother would not have died" (John 11:32). One of the least helpful ways that we deal with death is through blame. We blame ourselves, blame others, blame circumstances, and blame God. It's bewildering to watch a desperately ill friend waste away in spite of our tears and sincere prayer. "Where is God? Couldn't He have stopped this?"

I'll give Mary credit for this: She chided Jesus, not behind His back, but to His face. (I've noticed that the psalmist David did that a lot in the Psalms, as well.) How did Jesus respond when His friend Mary 'if-onlyed'

Him? He didn't go sit under a palm tree and pout. Rather than getting angry at Mary, He got angry at death. *When Jesus saw her weeping and saw the other people wailing with her, a deep anger welled up within him, and he was deeply troubled ... Jesus wept. (John 11:33 NLT, 35 NIV).*

When the friends of Lazarus saw the tears, compassion, and anger of Jesus, they sang their part in the "if-only" choir. "He cares and He can, so why in the world didn't He heal Lazarus?" The thing about if-only's is they tend to cement you into the past. Jesus didn't let the 'if-onlys' stop Him. He strode tearfully to the grave of Lazarus to deliver death an angry knockout punch.

What can I learn from Mary and Jesus? First, be honest with God. He's not intimidated by my "If only You..." statements. Second, be open to what God may do, even if it doesn't fit my formula or timetable. And third, I can stay close to Jesus. He may even trump my "If only You..." with His own "What if I..."

Life-action: Think of one "If only..." that tends to hold you in the past and totally let go of it, trusting God to trump death with life.

65

GRATEFUL DEAD

IT'S NOT TOO LATE for a new life.

JOHN 11:39-47

Jesus arrived in Bethany too late. Four days too late. Standing before His friend's tomb He commanded something that sounded shocking and ridiculous to the onlookers. "Roll away the stone." *But Martha, the dead man's sister, protested, "Lord, he has been dead for four days. The smell will be terrible" (John 11:39b, NLT).*

As some friends put their backs to the heavy stone, Jesus told Martha *"Did I not tell you that if you believed, you would see the glory of God?" (John 11:40).* The glory of God is a person who is alive with a miraculous new life. The glory of God, the bright splendor of God, is that He offers a kind of life that trumps death.

Before Jesus spoke to His entombed friend, He spoke to the Father, asking Him to release a miraculous burst of eternal aliveness. *When he had said this, Jesus called in a loud voice, "Lazarus, come out!" (John 11:43).* Imagine the shock of the incredulous doubters who saw an embalmed and wrapped Lazarus sit up on his cold stone ledge and then try to walk, or hop, into daylight. Jesus involved willing spectators in the

Lazarus miracle a second time when He said, *"Take off the grave clothes and let him go" (John 10:44b).*

This story teaches some important things about God's aliveness. First, I see in this story that it's not too late for God to bring life into our dead places. Is God calling out to something dead in you? A dead part of your body? A stiff marriage? A hopeless financial situation? A departed dream? Something you once pictured yourself doing that you've given up on? *You* may think it's too late, but *He* doesn't.

Second, God may ask me to play a part in someone's new life miracle. He may want me to be a stone-roller or a grave-clothing-remover. Only God can give new life, but He might want me to be His accomplice. He might ask me to do something ridiculous.

Third, don't expect everyone to be enamored with the idea of new life. Some of the spectators marveled, but others ran immediately to the religious leaders and tattled. Instead of rejoicing, the clergy fretted. *"What do we do now?" they asked. "This man keeps on doing things, creating God-signs" (John 11:47b, MSG).* Wow. Some people ignore God-signs. New life (life as it should be and could be) may appear to threaten life-as-it-is.

Life-action: Invite God again (the Bible says "keep asking") into a dead area in your life, and tell Him that if He gives life, you'll become one of His best stone-rollers.

66

LIFE AND DEATH

WE ALL NEED a life-savior.

Job 11:48-57

I was ten years old when my dad, who was a logger, pointed out a big white house on a hill near McMinnville, Oregon. Dad said, "The man who owned that house was a logger who saved his son by pushing him out of the way when a log came rolling down the hill toward them. The boy was saved, but the dad was crushed and killed."

It made me think of how Jesus came to give His life in my place. Not everyone sees Jesus in that light. The Jewish leaders saw potential death when they looked at Jesus and His miracles. *"If we let him go on like this, everyone will believe in him, and then the Romans will come and take away both our place and our nation" (John 11:48).*

At that point, the religious leaders decided to save the nation and its citizens by murdering Jesus and quashing His "kingdom of God" revolution. Little did they know that Jesus already planned to save the nation—and the world—by *giving* His own life. Oddly enough, both parties agreed that the death of one person could bring life to many people.

Anyone who lives to old age will probably have had their life saved by someone once or twice. A doctor. A parent. A fireman. A policeman.

A friend. I was hit by a car when I was seven years old. My mom saw it happen, screamed, and fainted. My dad ran out, scooped up my bloody body, and raced me to the hospital. He and the doctors saved me.

Sometimes there is only room for one savior in a given situation. The church leaders of Jesus' day pictured themselves as the 'intellectually and socially superior' saviors of their nation. I wonder. Do I ever pick myself as primary savior without realizing what I've done? "Move over Jesus. This is a bad situation, and I need to fix it."

There is only one primary Savior…Jesus, the Son of God. But He has also given me the high privilege of laying down my life for others in His name.

Life Question: Has anyone ever saved your life? Express your thankfulness and send a note or say a prayer.

67
THIEF

JESUS CARES about you and your life.

JOHN 12:1-11

Six days before He was executed, Jesus came to visit His friends, Mary, Martha, and their resurrected brother, Lazarus at their home in Bethany. When Jesus arrived, Mary lovingly poured out on His feet some very expensive perfume.

When she did this, Judas went berserk. *"Why wasn't this perfume sold and the money given to the poor? It was worth a year's wages."* *He did not say this because he cared about the poor but because he was a thief; as keeper of the money bag, he used to help himself to what was put into it.* (John 12:4-6)

Perhaps that perfume was Mary's retirement savings. According to Judas, it was worth a year's worth of wages. (The median household income last year in the United States was $62,175. Can you picture yourself giving away, unrequested, $62,175?)

I can almost hear his voice: 'Are you *kidding* me? This perfume could have been sold and given to Habitat for Humanity or Goodwill! Think how many starving kids overseas this money could have fed!"

He was a thief. But he didn't just take money, he took aliveness. The Bible tells us that *the love of money is a root of all kinds of evil (1 Timothy*

6:10). The root of Judas's greed had wrapped its tentacles around his soul. Love for money had crowded out the love of God—and love of God's people—from his heart.

What a contrast! As Mary embalmed the Lord, Judas embezzled from Him. As the aroma of her worship filled the room, Judas's attitude stank it up. For every Little Red Riding Hood of life, there's a Big Bad Wolf of death right around the bend. For every life-giver, there is a life-robber.

Jesus said, 'If a person gains the whole world and loses his or her soul (life), it is a net loss.' Had Judas heard Him say that? Almost certainly. But had he believed it? I don't think so.

I remember counseling a husband and wife whose marriage was on the rocks. He claimed that his wife was overspending. After looking at the data, it appeared to me that he was very selfish while she was thrifty and financially conservative. He was the one who was overspending. Overspending on himself. I'll never forget him yelling, "When she spends my money, she's spending my life." Little wonder the marriage was dying. One of them was a life-thief.

Please, Lord, let me be more like Mary and less like Judas.

Life Challenge: Can you picture yourself spending $60,000 to say "I love you" to Jesus?

68

HINDSIGHT

DON'T BE CONFUSED by setbacks. Life wins.

JOHN 12:12-19

I don't think I'll ever forget the 2015 Super Bowl: Seahawks vs. Patriots. Like many other west-coasters, I was rooting for Seattle. Late in the fourth quarter, it looked like Seattle's 'top-team-two-years-in-a-row-dream' was dead. Then they scored two touchdowns in less than a minute, and after one of the most amazing catches in football history, they found themselves at the two-yard line, ready to score the winning touchdown. I'm sure the Seahawk players were preparing a Gatorade shower for coach Carroll at that point.

That is kind of how it was for Jesus and His team of twelve. Fulfilling prophecies, He rode a donkey through a cheering throng in Jerusalem. He had recently raised Lazarus from the dead, and His support had reached a tipping point. In football terms, it was first and goal. Judas thought Jesus should run the ball up the middle. But much to Judas's dismay, Jesus passed and was intercepted, just like the Seahawks. Forget the Gatorade. Forget the new government. Forget winning.

At first his disciples did not understand all this. Only after Jesus was glorified did they realize that these things had been written about him and that they had done these things to him (John 12:16).

What was done to Jesus in the next few days fulfilled scriptural prophecies in great detail. All twelve disciples must have missed the prophetic message in Isaiah 53. *He was oppressed and treated harshly... his life was cut short in midstream. He had done no wrong ... But he was buried like a criminal; he was put in a rich man's grave (Isaiah 53:7-9, NLT).*

It looked like death won. (Sorry for the analogy, New England Patriots fans.) The truth is, however, that first-century game was rigged. Indeed, after the Lord's resurrection, the disciples realized that the last second interception from hell had been part of God's plan. Heaven allowed Satan to think that he had won, and the Lord's disciples to think they had lost. At this point, of course, the football analogy breaks down. A replay of the 2015 Super Bowl will not change who won. But Christ's resurrection changes everything.

God's amazing plan is summed up in the old hymn *Crown Him with Many Crowns:* "...Who came eternal life to bring and lives that death may die." His death killed my death. Yes, death may have won a battle that dark day, but Life won the war.

Life Challenge: Can you think of one negative situation you're dealing with where it looks like death is winning? Remember, Easter says "Life wins!"

69

TWO WAYS OF LIFE

UNDERSTAND two kinds of life.

JOHN 12:20-30

Facing death head-on, Jesus moved toward Jerusalem *with an iron will (Luke 9:51, TLB)*. Being careful not to talk over the heads of His disciples, Jesus used a simple botanical illustration to show how letting go of His life would bring life to many others.

"*Listen carefully: Unless a grain of wheat is buried in the ground, dead to the world, it is never any more than a grain of wheat. But if it is buried, it sprouts and reproduces itself many times over*" (John 12:24, MSG). A seed that dies precedes a plant that lives and reproduces. In view of that fact, Jesus challenged His followers to follow His example: "*The man who loves his life [**psuche**] will lose it, while the man who hates his life [**psuche**] in this world will keep it for eternal life [**zoe**]*" (John 12:25).

Hates his psuche? What in the world does that mean? For starters, in that culture "hates" sometimes meant "loves less." The Master warns that if we don't value *zoe* life above *psuche* life, we lose in the long run.

As we have noted earlier in this book, Jesus talked about two kinds of life: *Psuche*, a life destined to die, and *zoe*, a deeper, longer life, eternal and immovable.

In his book, *Selling Water by the River,* the author uses a clever illustration to explain the importance of putting *zoe* first. If I have five numbers - four zeros and one one - I can arrange them to come up with a value ranging from 0001 to 1000. The key to greater value is to get the 1 (*zoe*) before the zeros (*psuche*). The key to experiencing deep, unending life is putting *zoe* first.

That helps me appreciate even more the motive behind Jesus' decision to set His face toward Jerusalem and death. "The good shepherd lays down his life (*psuche*) for the sheep" (John 10:11). He let go of His life (*psuche*) so that whoever believes in Him will "have eternal life (*zoe*)" (John 3:16b).

I wonder if I would experience more of the reality of *zoe* life now if I gave 75 dollars to someone in need today instead of buying that fishing rod I want?

Life Challenge: Think of one way you can put the 1 before the 0 today.

70

WHAT KIND OF DEATH

ASK JESUS about life and death.

John 12:31-36

Years ago, when Michael Jordan was racking up wins in professional basketball, "I want to be like Mike" was a common saying. In other words,
"I want a 40-inch jump reach...I want to be an elite athlete...I want to
be popular...I want to be rich."

I doubt that anyone who saw Jesus gasping for air on the cross
thought just then, "I want to be just like Him!" His feet were more than
three feet off the ground, but it wasn't pretty.

Although few present at Golgotha cheered or felt drawn to God on
that dark day, multiplied millions would do so in years to come. *"But I,
when I am lifted up from the earth, will draw all men to myself." He said
this to show the kind of death he was going to die (John 12:32-33).*

What kind of death did Jesus die? He died a brutal death, a criminal
death. What's more, He died *your* death and *my* death. Knowing that
ultimate death is separation from God, Jesus absorbed our sin and was
separated from God for three days—so that you and I could be connected to God forever.

His being "lifted up" makes sense to me now, but it didn't to His listeners. Most of the people who understood that He was talking about death by crucifixion wondered how He could even hint that He was the promised Messiah—if He knew He was going to be executed.

The crowd responded, "We understood from Scripture that the Messiah would live forever. How can you say the Son of Man will die? Just who is this Son of Man, anyway?" (John 12:34, NLT). When God answers one question, it usually raises two more. Do you ever ask God questions? Does He answer? If so, do you usually like His answer?

> *Then Jesus told them, "You are going to have the light*
> *just a little while longer. Walk while you have the light,*
> *before darkness overtakes you" (John 12:35a).*

In other words, Jesus was saying, "Just stay close to Me and I'll turn the light on when you need it. I'll answer your questions at just the right time."

I need to remember that today. Maybe you do, too.

Life Question: Could asking questions be a form of prayer? What questions would you ask Jesus if He were standing beside you right now? And by the way, He really is.

71
PRAISE OF MEN

LIVE for an audience of One.

JOHN 12:37-43

At some point during my sophomore year of high school, I went AWOL, turning away from my family and their faith. To me, it seemed apparent that I would not be popular with the people I admired (gifted athletes and pretty girls) unless I got rid of the Christian ball and chain I'd been dragging around since childhood.

Over a three-year period, I walked away from God, heart-first. My head followed my heart and I soon came to the conclusion that Christianity was a man-made religion. Late in my senior year, confused and depressed, I tried to believe in God again. I tried reading the Bible, but the words that seemed to shine with revelation when I was a young boy now appeared to be nothing but ink on paper.

What made me blind? What keeps people from seeing and moving toward God-light? What blinded so many of the people who heard and saw Jesus? What kept them from seeing His *"cascading brightness?" (John 12:41, MSG)*.

Revelation requires information. That is a head issue. Revelation also requires courage. It requires a willingness to please God even when it displeases those around you. And that is a heart issue. Trusting Christ and following Him courageously takes grey matter and backbone. The concrete of faith needs the rebar of courage. Fear of man caused many in the Lord's audience to wimp out with a head-only faith.

> *Because of the Pharisees they would not confess their faith for fear they would be put out of the synagogue; for they loved praise from men more than praise from God (John 12:42-43).*

Who is in your grandstand? Who are you trying to please? Your fellow workers? Your kids? Your spouse? Your parents? The 'gifted athletes and pretty girls'?

Even when I couldn't see any proof of God's existence as a seeker in high school, the light of revelation was all around me. Light is light, even if you don't see it. The moment I took off the blindfold of people-pleasing, I began to see His reality. Because my heart was right, I saw the light.

Life-action: Finish this sentence: "Because I love God's approval more than the approval of other people, I will…."

72

SAVED

THE SAVIOR CAME to save your life.

JOHN 12:44-47

I remember stealing several cases of beer out of the back of a truck when I was in high school. The truck had been parked on a dark back street. If it had been parked on Main Street under a streetlight, we would have stayed away. Jesus said that some people love darkness (John 3:19). I did that night.

> *"I have come as a light to shine in this dark world, so that all who put their trust in me will no longer remain in the dark. I will not judge those who hear me but don't obey me, for I have come to save the world and not to judge it" (John 12:46-47, NLT).*

Jesus came to *save* people. That is the word He used (vs. 47) when He described His reason for showing up on earth. The word *save* (Greek *eksodzo*) is translated in the Bible as "saved, made whole and healed." To *save* means to lead out of darkness, death, and destruction into light, life, and salvation.

One time the Jewish religious leaders blasted Jesus for healing a crippled man during a Sabbath-day church service. Here is His reply to His critics: *"I have a question for you. Does the law permit good deeds on the Sabbath, or is it a day for doing evil? Is this a day to save life or to destroy it?" (Luke 6:9, NLT).*

Jesus equated saving life with doing good. Read verse nine again. The Lord equated destroying life with doing evil. Legalistic, man-made, ungracious religion actually does the evil one a favor, because it destroys lives. Religion often gets off track when religious people see themselves as the *prosecution* instead of joining in on God's defense team, actively defending and saving lives. Jesus came to help and heal and make broken people whole.

Aren't you glad? This boy is!

Life-action: Think back over your life and remember a time when you did something wrong in the dark. Thank God you didn't go to jail ... or thank Him that you did.

73
FOLLOW DIRECTIONS

FOLLOW DIRECTIONS to a better life.

JOHN 12:48-50

"*For I did not speak of my own accord, but the Father who sent me commanded me what to say and how to say it. I know that his command leads to eternal life*" *(John 12:49-50a).* Jesus followed directions given by His Father, and the Father directed Him to give us directions.

Like most men, I'm not good at asking for directions—and even worse at following printed instructions. Just recently, however, I forced myself to follow directions carefully, and painstakingly assembled an insulated metal dog kennel, rivets and all. Slowing down from my normal fast, impatient pace, I absorbed the instructions, and ended up with a deep inner satisfaction and two happy dogs. Following instructions yields rewards.

"*And I know his instructions lead to eternal life; so whatever he tells me to say, I say!*" *(John 12:50, TLB)* Jesus said what He said, and did what He did, so He could point the way to unending life. You and I can end up there IF we follow directions. If we don't, we'll be lost.

"There is a judge for the one who rejects me and does not accept my words; that very word which I spoke will condemn him at the last day" (John 12:48).

Jesus: "I gave you clear directions to life (through my words and deeds), but if you don't follow the directions, you'll end up at a *dead* end."

Life Question: Do you believe that every word Jesus spoke "leads to eternal life"? If so, does that affect how you read the Bible and how often you read the Bible?

74
THINK

BE CAREFUL TO THINK like Jesus, not like Judas.

JOHN 13:1-5

On the threshold of His arrest and crucifixion, Jesus shared a Passover supper with the twelve. During the course of that meal, He demonstrated the depth and longevity of His love for them by washing their feet in humble service. *During supper the devil had already suggested to Judas Iscariot, Simon's son, that this was the night to carry out his plan to betray Jesus (John 13:2, TLB).*

Judas sat on the devilish suggestion like a mother robin sits on an egg. Life and death dined together. Jesus and Judas both had plans to carry out; Jesus had a plan for giving life, and Judas had a plan for taking it away. If Judas were to write a book, it might be called *The Devil Driven Life.*

After that, he poured water into a basin and began to wash his disciples' feet, drying them with the towel that was wrapped around him (John 13:5). Jesus was foot-washing; Judas was back-stabbing. Jesus washed dusty, stinky "world-think" from the feet of His disciples. I wonder if He scrubbed Judas extra hard?

What an amazing scene! The Creator washing the feet of His creation.

What glory! What majesty! When did I get immunized to the shocking beauty of divine redemption?

I asked on Facebook what my friends thought of when they heard the words "Jesus and Judas," and received a number of interesting answers. *Good and bad. Sweet and sour. Life and death. Light and dark. Lover and deceiver. Grace and greed. Smart and dumber.*

This account brings so many questions to my mind! When did Judas start thinking wrong? When did he start living wrong? Did he repent before he committed suicide? And then this question: Do I ever think like Judas? A lot or a little?

In response to my 'Jesus and Judas' question, my friend Nita answered, "I think of the fight within each of us. I want to be more of Jesus, less of Judas." Me too, because how you think plays a large part in determining how you live and how you die, and then w.

Life Challenge: Jesus and Judas demonstrated grace and greed. Monitor your thoughts today. Are you thinking like Jesus or Judas?

75
ACHILLES HEEL

LET GOD REVEAL where you are vulnerable.

John 13:6-17

Standing at the threshold of His death, Jesus knelt and served His disciples, humbly washing their toes, soles, ankles, heels and…their Achilles tendons.

In Greek mythology, a woman named Thetis took her young son Achilles by the ankles and dipped him upside down in the magical River Styx. The water of the Styx gave him Superman-like invulnerability. But Thetis didn't baptize Achilles *completely*. His heels remained dry. Achilles grew up to be a great warrior, but one day a poisonous arrow launched by an enemy hit him in his heel and killed him.

Twelve disciples with twenty-four heels were present in the upper room at the last supper. When the twelve saw Jesus do what a lowly servant normally did, the cat got their tongues. All except Peter, who put his foot in his mouth. 'No way Lord.'"

Jesus gave Peter no choice, so he asked Jesus to pour the whole bucket of water on his head. 'You've already showered,' Jesus said, 'when you listened to my teachings and let My words wash your mind. Just let Me get this smudge on your heel.'

Even Superman was vulnerable—to Kryptonite. And the Lord's men were vulnerable too. First, they had a tendency to *not* do what they knew they should do. *"Now that you know these things, you will be blessed if you do them" (John 13:17).* "Serve others," Jesus said. They knew they should, but there is a vast Grand Canyon between knowing and doing. Second, they had a tendency to project their expectations onto God. *"No," said Peter, "you shall never wash my feet." Jesus answered, "Unless I wash you, you have no part with me" (John 13:8).*

There was some poisoned thinking in Peter's mind. Indeed, in all of His disciples' minds. Moments before, they had been arguing about who would be vice president in the Lord's cabinet. Surely God would do it their way. 'God is pretty wild, but I think we can train Him and bring Him into line.' Not so! The real and living God is not a manageable deity.

Our great vulnerability, I believe, lies in knowing what is right but not doing it—or maybe in expecting God to do things the way *we* think He should. Either way, such wrong thoughts about God lead us into wrong and destructive paths in our lives.

You might call it our Achilles heel.

Life Question: What is your primary Achilles heel? Discuss it with God.

76
THE NIGHT

GOD IS THERE in your darkest night.

JOHN 13:18-38

So Judas left at once, going out into the night (John 13:30, NLT).

And what a night it was! For Jesus, the twelve, and especially for Judas. Hellish darkness eclipsed his soul that night.

Earlier in this book, I described a dark Halloween night when I was 16. A couple of delinquent friends and I had loaded the back of a Toyota pickup with basketball-sized pumpkins in various stages of rotting. We drove around town throwing them onto porches of innocent victims and watching them explode when they hit the deck.

At one house, five seconds after the bomb exploded, a burly man ran out the front door, screaming. I took off at a full sprint around his house and through his back yard. All of a sudden everything turned upside down. I ran full speed into a neck-high clothesline in the dark. I'm glad the police didn't catch us. I can just see someone watching a police lineup and saying, "It was the guy with the red horizontal line on the front of his neck." In retrospect, it's amazing that I didn't break my neck.

Evil comes alive at night. Darkness conceals. According to the National Crime Victimization Survey, approximately two-thirds (63.2 percent) of rapes and sexual assaults occur at night and 71 percent of motor vehicle thefts.

Yes, night *conceals*. But night also *reveals*.

The extent of Judas's corruption would be revealed before the next sunrise. Peter, who had promised to stand with Jesus no matter what, would be revealed as a nocturnal braggart. On that night, and three days later, God's heart would be revealed through Jesus like never before. Because God works the night shift, the same darkness that concealed man's evil revealed God's love.

When he [Judas] had left, Jesus said, "Now the Son of Man is seen for who he is, and God seen for who he is in him" (John 13:31, MSG). That night in the upper room, in Gethsemane, God would be clearly revealed for who He was and is—Love. Jesus went to the cross because Jesus is love personified.

Life Question: What dark night have you experienced, physically or spiritually? In hindsight, can you see that God was at work in your darkness?

77

HEART TROUBLE

ASK JESUS to lead you to life.

JOHN 14:1-14

Bearing down on the completion of His mission, Jesus spoke to His disciples about going to a special place that could only be reached a certain way. Thomas panicked. *"Lord, we don't know where you are going, so how can we know the way?" (John 14:5).*

Imagine yourself in your car in a large, unfamiliar city at twilight. You're following a city-dweller friend to his apartment, and you stay right on his tail because if you lose him, you're lost. Just then your dad, sitting in the back seat of your car, has a heart attack. You know there is a hospital somewhere nearby, so you honk at your buddy and he pulls over. You yell, "I think Dad is having a heart attack! Show me the way to the hospital!" At that moment, your friend actually becomes "the way" to the hospital for you.

For those wanting to go to the special place Jesus talked about, He is not only the life of that place, He is the way to that place.

Thomas felt like Jesus ran a yellow light and left the disciples stranded at the intersection facing a red light. Fortunately for the disciples, Jesus pulled over and waited on the side of the road until the light changed.

He waited because, like your friend from the city, He is the way to the place of life.

> *Jesus answered, "I am the way and the truth and the life. No one comes to the Father except through me"* (John 14:6).

If you prize life and pursue life, there is a place you want to reach and a way you need to go. Stay close to Jesus. If you do, you will always be moving toward the place where He shares eternal life with the Father. That place where you're headed is the very essence of ultimate, indestructible aliveness. And when you finally arrive, you'll see that Jesus is not only the way to get there, He is also the Life you receive when you get there. He is both the journey and the destination. He is *zoe* life.

Life Question: Is there any area of your life where you need to follow Jesus more closely? How can you do that?

78
LEAVE ME ALONE

COME ALIVE to the Spirit of God today.

John 14:15-31

"Leave me alone!" I said (or yelled) that a thousand times to my brother and three sisters when I was a kid.

"Don't leave me alone!" I said that to my dad when I was seven, just as our family walked through the front gates of Disneyland into a giant cloud of strangers. "Stay close to me," Dad said. I obeyed because I didn't want to be lost in the big D eternally. At that moment, the happiest place on earth looked pretty frightening to me.

When Jesus told His disciples that He would be leaving them, they were frightened, too. 'Stay close to Me and obey Me' Jesus said, *"and I will ask the Father, and he will give you another Counselor to be with you forever— the Spirit of truth. The world cannot accept him, because it neither sees him nor knows him. But you know him, for he lives with you and will be in you … On that day you will realize that I am in my Father, and you are in me, and I am in you (John 14:16,17,20).*

Jesus told His disciples that after He rose from the dead and led the way into a new dimension of aliveness, He would be with them through the Holy Spirit. 'Just as the Father was with me and within me through the Holy Spirit, I will be with you and within you through the Holy Spirit. I road tested this thing and it works very well. Mark my words, this is life!'

What made this intimate union possible was the Lord's death on the cross. *In just a little while the world will no longer see me, but you're going to see me because I am alive and you're about to come alive (John 14:19, MSG).* Because He came alive after being dead, we can do the same.

Jesus sent the Spirit to help us by showing us how to share Christ's eternal aliveness, starting now.

Invite the Holy Spirit to help you come alive today. Make a mental note to request the same thing from Him at least two more times today.

79
LIVING LIMBS

YOU CAN BRING JOY to God.

Jᴏʜɴ 15:1-8

My Grandpa Dixon had a farm with a cherry orchard and an apple orchard. It gave him pleasure to let his kids and grandkids take his tall step-ladder and fill buckets with cherries and boxes with apples.

I remember helping Gramps cut off branches. We pruned the apple trees back every few years so they would produce bigger, tastier apples. I also remember cutting a limb off a fruitful cherry tree. The limb harbored a basketball-sized nest of caterpillars, gorging themselves on leaves.

Just recently, I thought of helping Grandpa Dixon prune those trees when I read John 15: "*...My Father is the gardener. He cuts off every branch of mine that doesn't produce fruit, and he prunes the branches that do bear fruit so they will produce even more*" (John 15:1a-2, NLT).

What does Jesus mean when He says, "every branch of mine"? Was He talking about the 12 disciples and all who would claim to follow Him through the years? Or was He talking about individual branches or components of each of our lives, some of which may need to be pruned or cut off?

Exactly what kind of fruit is God the Gardener looking for in my life? It surely includes the fruit of the Spirit, detailed by Paul in his letter to the Galatians: *Love, joy, peace, patience, kindness, goodness, faithfulness, gentleness, and self-control (Galatians 5:22b-23a, NLT)*. That list of character traits sounds a lot like the character of Jesus.

Grandpa expected apples from apple trees and cherries from cherry trees. God expects Christlikeness from followers of Christ. Nothing pleased Gramps more than a bumper crop of cherries and apples—and nothing pleases God more than a bumper crop of Christlikeness from His branches. Remembering that truth reminds me to stay connected to Christ, and to let God remove any caterpillar nests from my limbs. Listen to Jesus: *"My true disciples produce bountiful harvests. This brings great glory to my Father" (John 15:8, TLB)*.

Life Challenge: Is there anything God would like to prune back or cut off in your life? Let Him. The gain will be more than worth the pain.

80

GIVE LIFE, GET JOY

GIVE LOVE, give life, get joy.

JOHN 15:9-17

When the eternal Son of God came to earth, He had already decided to give His life in order to kill our death. Fast approaching the day of His death, Jesus urged His disciples to remain in His love by obeying His commandments. His commandments are summed up like this: "Love the Father and love one another just like I did." The love He spoke of was *agape* love—undeserved, unconditional love.

The essence of *agape* love is putting another person's well-being higher on your priority list than you put your own happiness. If putting God and others first is rated on a scale of 1-10, then dying in someone's place is a 9.5, and dying in the place of someone who doesn't deserve to be loved is a flat out 10. Jesus did that for me, and for you. Then He asked each of us to follow His example and give up our lives in order to help others be more loved and more alive.

There might be two major ways to give up your life for the sake of God or others. One way is all at once, in some form of love-based martyrdom—perhaps rescuing someone at the cost of your own life. The other way is to die one decision at a time, one loving action at a time. (Like washing the dishes for Linda, when I'd rather watch a TV program.)

Jesus said that dying for others leads to great joy. I don't think He felt much joy in Gethsemane, yet the Bible tells us that *for the joy set before him, he endured the cross (Hebrews 12:2)*. What joy was that? The joy of pleasing His Father. The joy of providing a way for people like you and me to enter heaven. In the same way, if I sacrifice something I want for the sake of God or others, I bring joy to the Lord—a joy that will boomerang and come back to me.

In John 15:11 NLT, Jesus says, **"I have told you these things so that you will be filled with my joy. Yes, your joy will overflow!"** Notice how He calls the joy He wants for us *His joy*. There's nothing sweeter than His joy becoming my joy, too. That joy is my strength. Laying down my life brings joy to Jesus, to Father God, and to me. Eventually, that kind of joy will spill out and splash on everyone.

Life Challenge: Are you willing to watch today for a chance to give someone life and love? If so, expect joy.

81
LIFE TERM

CHOOSE your terms.

JOHN 15:18-25

Have you ever signed up for something on-line and had them ask you to read the "conditions" and agree to abide by them? The website won't let you advance unless you agree to their terms.

Did you know God has terms? He has terms for living, and we are studying life by looking through the eyes of Jesus and John.

> *"If you lived on the world's terms, the world would love you as one of its own. But since I picked you to live on God's terms and no longer on the world's terms, the world is going to hate you" (John 15:19, MSG).*

How would you like to live on God's terms? Do those terms appeal to you? What are they? They're certainly not the world's terms. Satan, who is called "the god of this world," convinced Adam and Eve to live on the world's terms. *Every man for himself! Me first! Grab all you can! Go for the gusto!* In the Lord's wilderness temptation, the evil one tried to persuade Jesus to circumvent God's terms for living as a sacrifice for sinful humanity. God's terms can be condensed into one word: *Love.* To expand that a little: *Every man for the other, and all for God.*

In college, I interviewed a wealthy, top-level executive of Tektronix, Inc. I asked him, "What makes free enterprise run, what is the fuel?" He smiled and said, "Selfishness." Is it love that makes the world go 'round? Yes and no. Selfishness, not love, motors the world system. But, love, not selfishness, made Jesus' world go around.

Just before He left, Jesus said to those He loved, "Remain in me," (John 15:1-8), "Remain in my love," (9-17) and 'Remain as a misfit in the world.' (18-25) That third *remain* stuck in their throats a little. "He's leaving. We're staying—stranded here in this hateful, selfish world."

Jesus wants His disciples in the world, but He doesn't want world-think in them. The boat is supposed to be in the water, but when the water gets in the boat, we have problems. The Christian is supposed to be *in* the world, but not *of* the world.

Here is where eternal life starts, right here, right now. The first part of a Christian's eternal life begins on this planet. Would you like to live the first part of your eternity on God's terms? It's challenging: Live an others-first life in a me-first world.

Life challenge: Look for at least one chance today to live on God's "you first" terms.

82
SPIRIT OF LIFE

THE HOLY SPIRIT is the life of God, given to us.

JOHN 15:26-16:15

Have you ever had your world shaken when someone left your life? Maybe that person suddenly died, turned away from you, moved away, or divorced you and left you lonely.

Eleven sad disciples felt that way when Jesus told them He was leaving and challenged them to *remain* in Him and in His love, even as they *remained* in a super-hostile world. Jesus didn't promise His followers thornless roses, but He did promise to send help.

Question: "And tell us again just *why* would You abandon us and leave us in such a situation? We thought we'd be ruling the world with You from Jerusalem by now. Lord, how are we going to tell the world the good news about Your life and Your love if the world hates us?"

Answer: *"When the Counselor comes, whom I will send to you from the Father, the Spirit of truth who goes out from the Father, He will testify about me ... it is better for you that I go away, because if I do not go, the Helper will not come to you. But if I do go away, then I will send him to you"* (John 15:26, NIV; John 16:7, GNT).

Question: "Yes, Lord, but...just how will this Helper You speak of help us down here in the middle of the battle?"

Answer: *"He will bring glory to me by taking from what is mine and making it known to you" (John 16:14).*

Just as blood brings life-giving oxygen to all flesh in our bodies, the Helper, the Holy Spirit, brings the words and life of God to our being. Earlier, Jesus said it this way: *"Men can only reproduce human life, but the Holy Spirit gives new life from heaven" (John 3:6, TLB).*

Christ-followers have a Helper in a hostile world. The Helper brings a timely word and the precious life of God from heaven to us.

Life challenge: Ask the Helper to bring you new life from heaven today.

83
QUESTIONS?

ASK QUESTIONS THAT HELP you stay young as you grow up.

JOHN 16:16-33

When my daughter Kara was three, she became a Gatling gun of questions. Worn out by her relentless inquisitiveness, I finally said, "No more questions for ten minutes." She paused, smiled, and then asked, "What's a question?"

One day Jesus stirred up a hornet's nest of questions with His disciples (John 16:17, MSG). He began to talk about leaving, about going somewhere they couldn't go. The disciples cast sidelong glances at each other with expressions that said, "What's He talking about?" A big transition was coming for them, and transitions—whether it's a new school, a new season, new experiences or a new relationship—always raise questions.

The disciples acted like kids, asking question after question. Studies have shown that kids ask ten times more questions than adults. Why do you suppose that is?

"What's going to happen when you leave?" they asked. He answered: *"You'll be sad, very sad, but your sadness will develop into gladness" (John 16:20b, MSG).* When they still didn't get it, Jesus gave them an example.

"When a woman gives birth, she has a hard time…. But when the baby is born, there is joy in the birth" (John 16:21, MSG).

'Bingo! Now we get it' (see verse 29). One question was answered for them, but hundreds more would rise up in the days ahead. Many of those questions would be answered when Jesus rose from the dead, when He ascended to heaven, and when they were filled with the Spirit at Pentecost. Some still haven't been answered—and won't be until Heaven.

Revelation must be like one of those time-release capsules of medicine. It comes in stages, bit by bit. As time goes on and we continue to walk in the Spirit, we realize things about God, about what God is doing, about ourselves, and about what God wants us to know and do. The understanding doesn't come all at once, and it doesn't always come when we want it, but He reveals truth to us in His wise timing, just when we need to know. I guess that's part of the eternal adventure. Eternity will be a huge treasure chest of questions and answers, adventures and discoveries.

I'm so glad God doesn't get annoyed at our questions! He is certainly more patient with me than I was with Kara. As time goes on, I hope to ask more questions along the lines of "What are You doing that I can be involved with?" and less questions along the lines of "How will You help me with what I am doing?"

Life Question: (Aha! Two more questions.) If you could ask Jesus one question today, what would it be? Will you wait for a time-released answer?

84

LIFE ON DISPLAY

CHECK OUT God's display.

JOHN 17:1-12

I have a friend who builds homes in seventeen cities, with a display home in each of those cities. Instead of just seeing pictures, potential buyers can walk into a model home and discover its quality and beauty for themselves. They can open cabinet doors, peer into corners, walk around the garage, and check out the smallest details.

In a similar way, God put His love and His life—He put Himself—on display in Jesus. The Bible word for this attractive display is "glory." To *glorify* is to express in a good light, to reveal the beauty and qualities of a person or thing.

After Jesus said this, he looked toward heaven and prayed: "Father, the time has come. Glorify your Son, that your Son may glorify you" (John 17:1). Then Jesus said to the Father, *"I spelled out your character in detail" (John 17:6, MSG).* What is God's character? First, God is love. The words "God" and "love" occur *together* 388 times in the Bible. Second, God is life—in its original and highest dimension.

God is life and God gives life. God is love and gives love. In love, He gave His life to us in Jesus. (Giving yourself—your life—to someone else is the essence of love.) We can see from the words of Jesus, recorded in John 17, that the Father gives life to the Son, who gives life to the Spirit, who gives life to us. Just as my builder friend invites interested people into his display home, God invites us into His loving aliveness, available to us, here and now.

Ten years ago, I found myself in a dark cave of depression.[1] My wife and several friends helped me take another look, a closer look, at God's self-display—His amazing, unearned love for me. What I saw saved my life.

And now, since I am alive in His aliveness, alive in His love, I can be a small part of God's display. I can speak hope to others. What Jesus prayed has come to pass: *"And my life is on display in them" (John 17:10b, MSG).*

Life Challenge: Take five minutes and read John 17. Be as attentive as you would if you were looking at a house you thought you might buy.

85
LOVE LIFE

FATHER GOD LOVES YOU just like He loves Jesus.

JOHN 17:13-40

In John 17, the cross was getting closer. Jesus spoke out loud to His Father about His followers and made several requests. He asked, on their behalf, for six things: joy, protection, purity, unity, uniqueness, and purpose. Then—thank God for this!—He extended that request to cover all who would believe in Him through the centuries because of their testimony.

Jesus went on to say that He brought the disciples into the Father-Son-Spirit circle of relationship *"...So that the world will know you sent me and will understand that you love them as much as you love me"* (*John 17:23b, TLB*).

That sentence stops me in my tracks. Jesus is reminding Himself, just before the cross, that the Father loves Him. And He is saying that the Father loves those that follow Him "as much as" He loves the Lord Jesus. I just now stopped and said out loud, "God loves me just like He loves Jesus." It almost sounds like heresy, but it lines up perfectly with Christ's prayer, and with John 3:16.

Bolstering Himself for His crucifixion, Jesus basically said three times to the Father, "You love Me." He put on His bullet-proof *I am loved* vest just before He charged hell to set captives free.

Perhaps you and I need to follow the Lord's example and remind ourselves over and over that the Father loves the Son, and that He loves equally all those who are in the Son. Literally and amazingly, if Christ is in me, then God loves me just as much as He loves His firstborn Son.

Jesus closed His intimate prayer with these words: *"I have made you known to them, and will continue to make you known in order that the love you have for me may be in them and that I myself may be in them"* *(John 17:26).*

Frankly, that staggers me.

The love the Father has for the Son can literally be in me as well.

Life Challenge: Write this note where you will see it. "God loves Jesus and me." Say it several times today.

86

THE CUP

JESUS SWALLOWED your sin.

JOHN 18:1-17

Have you ever had a colonoscopy? It isn't what I would call a picnic in the park. I've had five. The first one, some 30 years ago, found a pre-cancerous polyp in my colon. I watched on the screen as the surgeon clipped and cauterized the deadly polyp. Later the doctor said that given my family history, the surgery probably saved my life.

To clean my colon before the surgery, they gave me a gallon of soapy water to drink, and one hour to drink it. By the time I swallowed the last cup, I was gagging. The results of the procedure were sweet, but the cup was bitter.

As Jesus was being taken captive by soldiers and guards, He said to Peter *"Shall I not drink the cup which my Father has given me?" (John 18:11).*

What was the cup?

They arrested Jesus in an olive grove at the base of the Mount of Olives. That small orchard was called Gethsemane, a name which comes from the Hebrew words *gath* (press) and *shemen* (oil or wine): The Olive Oil Press. Here Jesus Christ was crushed and sweat blood before He bled life. That was His cup. That was the Father's bitter assignment for His beloved Son. His Son would be crushed so you and I could be made whole.

What was in the cup?

All of my sins. All of your sins. And the sins of Abraham Lincoln, Hitler, Stalin, and Osama bin Laden, as well the sins of child molesters (including some priests and ministers), assassins and suicide bombers. Sinless Jesus swallowed the filthy sewage of every sin ever committed. Can you even imagine drinking that?

I drank the awful cup the physician gave me so I could live longer. Jesus drank the putrid cup the Father gave Him so that I could live forever. Only love would do that.

Life Challenge: The next time you consider committing "a very small sin," stop and think before you do: Jesus will have swallowed that sin.

87
LIFE SENTENCE

ONE SENTENCE can change your life forever.

JOHN 18:18-24

Politics and religion are like oil and water. They don't blend well.

Under arrest, Jesus was taken to a religious, political circus. He stood first before Annas, the father-in-law of Caiaphas, the high priest. Annas bullied Jesus, bound him, and sent him to Caiaphas. *Caiaphas was the one who had told the other Jewish leaders, "It's better that one man should die for the people" (John 18:14, NLT).*

Wiley old Caiaphas thought he would take the bull by the horns, have Jesus arrested, turned over to the Romans, found guilty of sedition, and crucified. "It is better that one man should die for the people." That sentence is true. Caiaphas got it right. But he was wrong in thinking that handing a death sentence to Jesus was his clever, original idea. Actually, it was God's idea first.

Someone else thought it was his idea, too. Satan, **"the god of this world"** (2 Corinthians 4:4), was sure *he* had thought it up. He pulled the puppet strings on Annas, Caiaphas, Judas, and others, but in actuality, he was playing right into God's hands.

What does this say to me? First, as I mentioned earlier, politics and religion don't blend well. (Just think of Muslim terrorists) Next, it says that God is in control even when it looks like He isn't. It also reminds me that God gave His much-loved Son to die under my death sentence. It was He who came up with the amazing idea that one could die for many, taking their death sentence and giving them a life sentence. Here is that sentence: *"For God so loved the world that he gave his one and only Son, that whoever believes in him shall not perish but have eternal life"* *(John 3:16)*. That sentence changed my 'forever address!'

Life Question: Is there any area of your life where you sometimes imagine yourself to be in control? Take time today to deliberately yield control of that area to God because He loves you.

88

NOTHING BUT THE TRUTH

THE TRUTH IS, Jesus is not guilty. I am.

John 18:25-40

John had a court scene in mind when he wrote his gospel. The words *witness, truth*, and *testify* occur over and over in his book. You and I, the readers, join readers from all over the world, through over 2,000 years of history, to form the jury.

Jesus makes the statement "I tell you the truth" 30 times in the book of John. He not only says "I *tell* you the truth," He says, "I *am* the truth." Ironically, the One who was 'TRUTH personified' was accused of being a deceiver and a liar. Jesus didn't say much at His trial, but He did say this: *"If I said anything wrong, you must prove it. But if I'm speaking the truth, why are you beating me?" (John 18:23b, NLT).*

Jesus gave the real truth to His enemies, even though they strongly rejected it. *"You're from your father, the Devil, and all you want to do is please him. He was a killer from the very start. He couldn't stand the truth because there wasn't a shred of truth in him" (John 8:44, MSG).*

The religious leaders, claiming truth, were children of the father of lies. The disciples thought they were telling the truth when they said they'd stick with Jesus to the end. But the real truth is that they all ran for the high hills like a bunch of scared rabbits.

Peter had insisted he was telling the truth when he said he would never deny Jesus, even if he had to die for it. But by the time the rooster crowed the next morning, he had denied Jesus three times.

Pilate said "What is truth?", even as he deliberately condemned an innocent man to save his own job and his neck.

So, my fellow jury member, what is the truth? If Jesus is telling the truth, if He is the very embodiment of truth, then Pilate, Peter, the other disciples, Judas, the religious leaders, Satan, and you and I and Satan are all guilty.

The number one aim in all of life is to get on the right side of the truth. Reach out a hand to Jesus and He will pull you out of deception and darkness and re-establish your life in His truth. Forever and ever.

Life challenge: Listen to yourself as you say this out loud, "I owed a debt I could not pay. He paid a debt He did not owe."

89
NOT GUILTY

HE GAVE HIS LIFE to save my life.

JOHN 19:1-18

Several years ago, a group of men from our church went to the now-closed McNeil Island Correctional Center in Washington, where we were allowed to speak with inmates who wanted to talk. I had conversations with a number of men that day. About half of them basically said, "I am guilty, and I want to do better." The other half said, in essence, "I am innocent, and I shouldn't be in this prison at all."

When I talked with the warden later, I shared the gist of my conversations. He smiled and said, "Most of the men who say, 'I am guilty,' will one day be free and live productively in society. Most of the men who say, 'I am not guilty' will keep coming back here for most or all of their lives."

After talking with Jesus in today's reading, Pilate said, "He is not guilty." In spite of that, trying to appease the Jewish religious leaders, that highly political Roman official had Jesus flogged. Then he stood before those same leaders and said, *"I am going to bring him out to you now, but understand clearly that I find him not guilty" (John 19:4b, NLT).*

The religionists went bonkers. *"If you let this man go, you are no friend of Caesar. Anyone who claims to be a king opposes Caesar" (John 19:12b).*

In that instant, Pilate realized his neck was on the block. If the Jews rioted, he could be demoted, or if Caesar found out that Jesus broke the Roman law by calling Himself a king, Pilate would face being beheaded.

We all have the same battle going on within us today. It's a battle between self-preservation (saving my own life at all costs) and self-sacrifice (giving my own life for what is right, at all costs).

So who is actually on trial here? Is Jesus? Is Pilate? Is Judas? Are the disciples? Are the religious leaders? Am I? Are you? We all are. *For everyone has sinned; we all fall short of God's glorious standard (Romans 3:23, NLT).*

At the final judgment, when the Judge has me stand and make my plea, I hope to say, "I am guilty, Your Honor. And thank You, Your Honor, for the One who gave His life to save my life."

Life Challenge: Embrace self-giving today. See if you can catch yourself giving yourself to help others.

90

A SIGN

JESUS AND THE CROSS are signs for seekers.

John 19:19-22

Pilate had a notice prepared and fastened to the cross. It read: Jesus of Nazareth, the King of the Jews (John 19:19).

What caused Pilate to have these words fastened to the cross? The same people who blackmailed Pilate into issuing an order for the crucifixion of Jesus threw a fit when they saw the sign. They wanted Pilate to insert the words "HE SAID HE WAS" before the words "THE KING OF THE JEWS."

Why did Pilate write' 'THE KING OF THE JEWS"? Did Pilate's wife talk him into doing it? Did his guilty conscience compel him to stand by his five-letter title? Was there a tiny grain of faith embedded in his heart?

The message on the sign was written in three languages, including Aramaic, the common language among Jews—known across the world for their belief in one God. The notice also went forth in Greek and

Latin, the languages of Greece and Rome, two empires unsurpassed in jurisprudence and education.

"All roads lead to Rome" was a medieval statement referring to the Roman road system where all the empire's roads radiated out from the capital city. The statement is still used today to mean "everything leads to the center of things."

Was the notice posted on Christ's cross God's way of saying, "What is happening here is the center of things for all of mankind"? The Bible says that many Jews, as well as people from other nations, read the sign. I wonder how many Greek foreigners read it? The Roman soldiers surely read the Latin version. One day, the scriptures say, every knee will bow, and every tongue will confess that Jesus is 'Lord,' a common title for kings.

I got on my knees just now. I said, "Lord God, I'm not waiting until that day to bow. Thank You for Your signs of life. Thank You that people from every tribe and nation have seen the signs. Thank you for opening my eyes to the signs and to the King."

Life Challenge: Thank God for the cross and what it signifies.

91

DO YOU BELIEVE?

JOHN'S REPORT OF JESUS was accurate.

JOHN 19:23-45

We are nearing the completion of our slow walk through the gospel of John, a book about God, about life, and about you.

John doesn't beat around the bush; he even says this book *was* written for you. Speaking of himself, he says, *The eyewitness to these things has presented an accurate report. He saw it himself and is telling the truth so that you, also, will believe (John 19:35, MSG).*

The Spirit of God guided John as he wrote—and believe it or not, it was written all those years ago with *you* in mind. So I have a few questions for you.

Do you believe God knew you would read John's book (see John 20:31)?

Do you believe John told the truth and was accurate as he wrote the book (see John 19:35)?

Do you believe that Jesus' life and death fulfilled numerous specific prophecies written long before His birth (see John 19:24)?

Do you believe that Jesus paid your debts? "It is finished," (Jesus' final words on the cross, can be translated "Paid in Full." It is the term that was stamped on fully paid bills in that time and place.)

Do you believe the Good News of God's amazing, available aliveness? Paul, who once hunted down and imprisoned Christians, came to believe. A thief who spent several hours on a cross next to Jesus found faith. Nicodemus, who first came to Jesus under the cover of night, must have come to believe, since he came out of the closet and identified with Jesus in the full light of day.

Life Challenge: Because you believe, let someone know today.

92

MYSTERY

FIND YOUR STORY in life's mystery.

JOHN 20:1-14

Early on the first day of the week, while it was still dark, Mary Magdalene went to the tomb and saw that the stone had been removed from the entrance (John 20:1).

Mary, however, wasn't the only one in the dark that early Sunday morning. What had happened three days before made no earthly sense to the disciples.

So often, when God does something new, it begins as a mystery. Mary's deep devotion put her in a place where she would be the first to connect the initial pieces of the new 'puzzle.' At the resurrection, God said, "Ladies first," and Mary joyfully shared her experience.

So Peter and the other disciple started for the tomb (John 20:3).

Recently, I told a group of men that I was born in a hospital in McMinnville, Oregon. Then I asked where each of them was born. They came from all over the map, east, west, north, south. They all had a birthplace…but none of us were born in a graveyard.

The birthplace of the Christian faith, a tomb, was the last place you'd expect to find life. When it comes to God, one learns to expect the unexpected.

Peter ran into the tomb and John looked into the tomb. Different people approach a miracle in different ways. Jesus' body was gone, but the cloth that had covered His head was folded and lying near where His body had been placed. This seemed to say to Peter and John that the Lord's body had not been stolen. It left things open-ended. As the famous news commentator Paul Harvey used to say, "And now, the rest of the story."

At least three people were raised from the dead by Jesus. Now the One who resurrected others was Himself resurrected. Mystery became reality. And that mystery, now history, has become part of God's story and my story.

Life challenge: Write down one piece of the puzzle of life that is a mystery to you. Ask God to shed some light on it.

93

"I WILL NOT BELIEVE UNLESS..."

GET READY TO GO higher in your faith.

JOHN 20:15-25

*So the other disciples told him, "We have seen the Lord!"
But he said to them, "Unless I see the nail marks in his
hands and put my finger where the nails were, and put
my hand into his side, I will not believe it." (John 20:25).*

Mary had touched Jesus after His resurrection. Peter and John went to
His open tomb. Other disciples had seen the Lord in various places. Some
of them had been together in a house behind a locked and dead-bolted
door when Jesus appeared in their midst. What was their faith level at
this point? It probably varies, but I wonder whether the corporate faith
level was about a five on a scale of one to ten.

I think of faith as a two-story house with a basement. Thomas, ab-
sent when the Lord came through the walls, was in the basement of faith,
refusing to believe unless he touched the Evidence. The other disciples
were in a room on faith's ground floor, believing, somewhat. Weeks later
they would all be in an upper room with open windows.

My faith level has ranged over time from the basement to the upper room. In the course of our lives, faith may not necessarily remain settled and final. But neither will doubt.

There are two main words for doubt in the New Testament. One word means *dialog*. It pictures an inner dialog that is in process and will eventually be resolved as belief or unbelief. The other word is the root of our word *meteorite*. This implies that faith hasn't landed yet; it's still up in the air like a meteor. A doubting person's heart and mind can yet hit the ground in the land of belief, or in the land of unbelief.

I'm no stranger to doubt, and I've found myself in faith's dark basement several times through the years. I'm glad Jesus came to the first-story Christians, to Thomas in the basement, and via the Holy Spirit, to the believers in the upper room. After finding me in the basement many years ago, He's come to me in all three rooms.

Life challenge: Is your faith underground, at ground level or in the second story today? Are you headed up or down? Ask God to help you climb the steps to a higher story of faith.

94
STOP DOUBTING

GOD MOVES toward honest doubt with evidence.

John 20:26-31

Most of the eleven disciples had seen Jesus since His resurrection. It had been eight days since He suddenly appeared among a group of them. When told of the encounter, Thomas responded with doubt. He just couldn't buy into their excited account, and declared that he wouldn't believe until he saw, heard, and touched Jesus. He needed tangible evidence. His faith had been weak for a week.

> *Eight days later the disciples were together again, and this time Thomas was with them. The doors were locked; but suddenly, as before, Jesus was standing among them. "Peace be with you," he said. Then he said to Thomas, "Put your finger here, and look at my hands. Put your hand into the wound in my side. Don't be faithless any longer. Believe!" (John 20:26-27).*

Instantly, faithless Thomas became a believer. He fell at Jesus' feet and cried out, *"My Lord and my God!" (John 20:28, NLT).* Those five words had historical significance. During the writing of John, the Emperor Domitian required his subjects to refer to him as *Dominus et Deus* (Lord and God), the exact phrase that Thomas used to cry out to Jesus.

> *Then Jesus told him, "You believe because you have seen me. Blessed are those who believe without seeing me"* (John 20:29, NLT).

The Bible says that more than five hundred people saw tangible Jesus after He rose from the dead. And since that time, perhaps more than five hundred million people have used their spiritual eyes to see Him. One day, each of us will stand before Him as Thomas did on that day. Until then, we can encounter and experience Him by means of our quickened spiritual senses.

I haven't seen what Thomas saw. I haven't heard or touched Jesus in the flesh. But I have believed. I will be among the millions who will one day stand before Him, in the flesh, as Thomas did. And even though the throng will be vast, I know that He will treat me like one-in-a-million.

Life Question: Aren't you glad that God moves toward good-hearted doubt, and not away? If so, tell Him.

95

UNCERTAIN?

JESUS CAN BRING CERTAINTY to your uncertainty.

JOHN 21:1-14

Jesus died on the Jewish Passover. Fifty days later, during the Jewish celebration of Pentecost, a room full of His Spirit-filled followers burst out of the upper room onto the crowded streets of Jerusalem, boldly sharing God's good news.

The 47 days between Jesus' resurrection and Pentecost were days of uncertainty for His disciples. They had never been taught about the second coming of Christ. What would they do and where should they go from there?

Seven of them went fishing. They fell back on what was familiar, as we all tend to do in times of uncertainty. They were all trying to figure out what Christ's resurrection meant to their future. They needed food, money, security, and direction. After fishing all night long, however, they hadn't netted a single fish. Was God saying, "Don't go backward, go forward"?

When the sun came up, Jesus was standing on the beach, but they didn't recognize him (John 21;4 MSG). The stranger yelled, "Cast your net off the right side of the boat and see what happens." He spoke with such authority that they obeyed. Instantly, a giant school of large fish swam into their net. It was a déjà vu miracle, just like the supernatural sign Jesus had performed when He initially enlisted them.

Peter jumped out of the boat and swam for the beach to meet the Lord. Jesus had some fish sizzling over a fire and invited the men to bring a few of the fresh-caught fish to add to those already cooking.

Standing around the fire and eating fish with Jesus must have been a surreal experience. Those seven men must have felt they were straddling the line that separates the natural from the supernatural. Actually, we all are.

Even when we are feeling uncertain and undecided, even when things seem blurry and hazy, we're just the width of a boat—one act of obedience—away from divine provision, confirmation, and renewed direction.

Life Challenge: Is there any place in your life where you have fallen away from Christ's call – the special assignment He has for you? If so, ask Him to re-enlist you.

96
RE-ENLIST IN LIFE

JESUS CAME TO GIVE us abundant aliveness in our relationship with God and with others.

JOHN 21:1-14

Jesus had a private matter to settle with Peter, and He chose to take care of that with the others listening in. He had come to the shores of the Sea of Galilee near where Peter and six other disciples were fishing. After they finished eating fish tacos, Jesus asked Peter, *"Simon, son of John, do you love me more than these?" (John 21:15)*. We don't know for sure what Jesus pointed to when He said, "more than these." Were "these" the boats and nets? The fish? My guess is "these" were the other six disciples.

Before Jesus was arrested and murdered, Peter told Jesus: "Even if *these* other disciples bail on you, I won't." Then Peter, under pressure, denied three times that he even knew Jesus. Here by the sea the risen Christ publicly probed Peter three times with the question, "Do you love Me?" Peter got the point, and it was a sharp one.

Perhaps Peter needed to re-enlist. Did he feel broken and devastated after failing the Lord so dramatically? Was he thinking seriously about returning to his former occupation? Were the other six disciples ready to hand in their two-week notice as well? If so, Jesus came to convince Peter and the others that if we love God, ("Do you love Me?"), and then love others, ("more than these?"), we can fail *forward.*

Love is both vertical and horizontal. The ten commandments are horizontal (loving others) and vertical (loving God). The Bible, in a nutshell, says, "Love the Lord your God..." (vertical) and "love your neighbor as yourself" (horizontal).

Like God's love, God's life has a horizontal and vertical dimension. At the beach, Jesus restored Peter's vertical aliveness, his connection with God, and his horizontal aliveness, his connection with others. God's life, offered to us in Christ, makes us more alive with God and with others.

Two key verses in this living gospel speak of God's love (John 3:16) and God's life (John 10:10). Aren't you glad that Jesus came to fill us with God's multidimensional love and life? That's the main message of the book of John.

Life Question: If Jesus asked you today, "Do you love Me more than these?" what might the "*these*" be?

97

AS FOR YOU...

AS FOR YOU...follow the Lord of Life.

JOHN 21:20-25

Jesus came to reveal God's gift of deep, unending aliveness, and to deliver that gift to us through His death and resurrection. That lift-gift is sourced in our vertical relationship with God and expresses itself through our horizontal relationship with others.

John's gospel—his account of God's aliveness wrapped in Jesus—ends with Jesus coming to His disciples' workplace—the sea—to make sure that they didn't confuse "making a living" with "living a life." He wanted them to remember the signs of life He had shown them over their three years of walking together.

Jesus helped Peter re-enlist, and then quietly informed him that his tenure on earth would end with martyrdom, just as the Lord's had. Tradition tells us that the big fisherman was eventually crucified, upside down, because he refused to do a re-run of his earlier denial of Christ.

When Peter caught what Jesus was saying, he asked the Lord if his dear friend John would fare any better. "What about him, Lord?" Jesus replied, *"If I want him to remain alive until I return, what is that to you?" (John 21:22a).*

We make a mistake when we put the horizontal (our relationship with others) before the vertical (our relationship with God). Jesus gently chided Peter with the words, *"As for you, follow me." (John 21:22b)* Following Jesus is, at its essence, an individual thing. You *shouldn't* follow Jesus because someone else does, and you *should* follow Him even if and when no one else does. When He returns, we will stand before Him individually, not as couples or groups.

Maybe you've allowed your horizontal relationships to have a negative effect on your relationship with God. Maybe you've lived through a painful church split, been divorced by someone who claimed to be a Christ-follower or abandoned by someone who should have helped you and stayed with you.

Jesus didn't say, "Get over it." He said, tenderly but firmly, to Peter, to you, and me, **"As for you, follow me."**

Life Challenge: Is there a person you would ask the Lord about, "What about him? What about her?" Hear the voice of the Living One: "As for you, follow Me."

CONCLUDING THOUGHTS

John's gospel—his account of God's aliveness wrapped in Jesus – is saturated with signs of life. My prayer is that you will follow those signs, and in doing so, become physically, mentally, socially, spiritually and eternally more alive.

"The signposts of GOD are clear and point out the right road. The life-maps of GOD are right, showing the way to joy." (Psalm 19:7-8)

REVIEW INQUIRY

Hey, it's Ken Johnson here.

I hope you've enjoyed the book, finding it both useful and fun. I have a favor to ask you.

Would you consider giving it a rating on Amazon or wherever you bought the book? Online book stores are more likely to promote a book when they feel good about its content, and reader reviews are a great barometer for a book's quality.

So please go to Amazon.com (or wherever you bought the book), search for my name and the book title, and leave a review. If someone gave you a copy of my book, then leave a review on Amazon, and maybe consider adding a picture of you holding the book. That increases the likelihood your review will be accepted!

Many thanks in advance,

Ken Johnson

WILL YOU SHARE THE LOVE?

Get this book for a friend, associate or family member!

If you have found this book valuable and know others who would find it useful, consider buying them a copy as a gift. Special bulk discounts are available if you would like your whole team or organization to benefit from reading this. Just contact info@muchmorealive.com or https://MuchMoreAlive.com.

WOULD YOU LIKE KEN JOHNSON TO SPEAK TO YOUR ORGANIZATION?

Book Ken Johnson Now!

Ken Johnson accepts a limited number of speaking and coaching engagements each year. To learn how you can bring his message to your organization, email info@muchmorealive.com or visit https://MuchMoreAlive.com.

ENDNOTES

1. Johnson, Ken. *When It All Comes Down It All Comes Down to This: Live in God's Love.* Ephraim Enterprises, 2019.

ABOUT THE AUTHOR

The Creator wired Ken Johnson to be an entrepre-
neur. Before he was ten, he was shoveling snow in
the winter and selling hand-picked wild blackber-
ries door-to-door in the summer. Ken graduated
in 1972 from George Fox University with a Bach-
elor of Science in Business Administration, and
then experienced seven years of rich productivity
as a businessman.

Surprisingly, Ken felt a divine nudge to leave
the business realm where he was thriving and become a minister. He
started by leading a little flock of thirty people, and years later he found
himself leading thousands.

Ken served on the Foursquare Church international Board, and on
the Foursquare Foundation Board for six years. The Foundation has
awarded more than $52,000,000 in grants to fruitful Christian leaders
and ministries throughout the world. Seeing tens of thousands of people
all over the world find new life in God shot adrenaline into Ken's soul.

In 2013, Ken, an avid outdoorsman, was diagnosed with Parkinson's
Disease. Ken handed the leadership of Westside Church (which is still
thriving) to his assistant, but he didn't retire. He 're-fired.' He continued
to speak various places and began to direct more and more of his energy
to mentoring leaders and writing.

Ken has published three books: *Life² – The Life You Were Created to
Live, When it All Comes Down it All Comes Down to This*, and *Signs of*

Life – God's Invitation to a Better, Stronger & Longer Life. Ken is preparing to publish a trilogy called *Your Wildest Dream*.

Ken's focus is helping people become more alive through his books and his blog: *Much More Alive*. Whether writing or speaking, Ken is a vibrant, adventurous storyteller who uses stories to open people's minds and unbridle powerful emotions. Nothing thrills Ken more than helping people become more prolific, more purposeful, more alive!

Ken Johnson can be reached at: https://MuchMoreAlive.com

Made in the USA
Coppell, TX
21 May 2020

26147461R10125